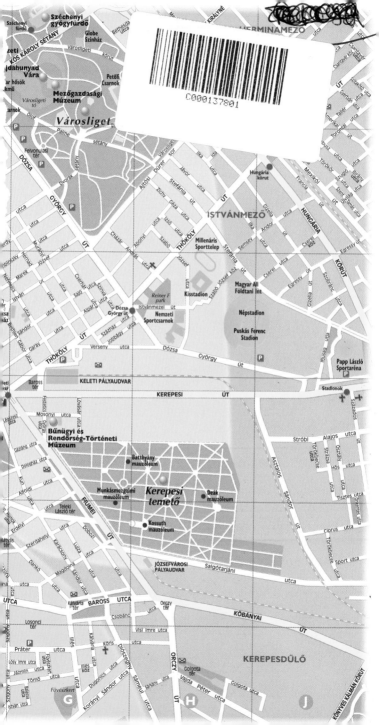

CITYPACK TOP 25
Budapest

ADRIAN PHILLIPS

If you have any comments or
suggestions for this guide
you can contact the editor at
Citypack@theAA.com

AA Publishing
Find out more about AA Publishing and the
wide range of services the AA provides by
visiting our website at www.theAA.com/travel

How to Use This Book

KEY TO SYMBOLS

✚	Map reference to the accompanying fold-out map	❓	Other practical information
✉	Address	▷	Further information
☎	Telephone number	ℹ	Tourist information
🕐	Opening/closing times	✋	Admission charges: Expensive (over 1,500Ft), Moderate (800Ft–1,500Ft), and Inexpensive (800Ft or less)
🍴	Restaurant or café		
🚆	Nearest rail station	⭐ Major Sight	★ Minor Sight
Ⓜ	Nearest subway (Metro) station	👣 Walks	🚌 Excursions
🚌	Nearest bus route	🛍 Shops	
⛴	Nearest riverboat or ferry stop	🎵 Entertainment and Nightlife	
♿	Facilities for visitors with disabilities	🍽 Restaurants	

This guide is divided into four sections

• **Essential Budapest:** An introduction to the city and tips on making the most of your stay.

• **Budapest by Area:** We've broken the city into six areas, and recommended the best sights, shops, entertainment venues, nightlife and restaurants in each one. Suggested walks help you to explore on foot.

• **Where to Stay:** The best hotels, whether you're looking for luxury, budget or something in between.

• **Need to Know:** The info you need to make your trip run smoothly, including getting about by public transport, weather tips, emergency phone numbers and useful websites.

Navigation In the Budapest by Area chapter, we've given each area its own colour, which is also used on the locator maps throughout the book and the map on the inside front cover.

Maps The fold-out map accompanying this book is a comprehensive street plan of Budapest. The grid on this fold-out map is the same as the grid on the locator maps within the book. We've given grid references within the book for each sight and listing.

Contents

Introducing Budapest

Since shaking off the last shackles of communism in 1991, Budapest has quickly developed into one of Europe's most enticing capitals. Boasting an exciting and elegant range of sights and styles, it has something to appeal to all tastes.

For much of its history, Budapest's was a tale of two cities. The famous Chain Bridge—the first permanent structure here to span the Danube—wasn't opened until 1849, and before that the river formed a barrier separating the communities on each side. The characters of Buda (to the west of the river) and Pest (to the east) remain very different to this day. Buda holds the palace and medieval Castle District, before giving way to leafy hills. Pest is the financial and commercial heart, home to the Parliament building, the business district and the main concentration of shops, restaurants and bars.

What makes Budapest an enchanting spot for a city break is the variety it offers. In any given day you're likely to encounter art nouveau mansions, a neo-Gothic church topped with vivid roof tiles and pastel medieval houses. You'll stroll Parisian-style boulevards and quaint cobbled alleys, relax in lush parks or paved squares, browse bustling markets or sprawling shopping malls, have cake in a *fin-de-siècle* coffee shop or a beer in a lively bar. And there's a plethora of museums and galleries.

Even during the Communist period, Hungary always leaned toward the West. It's a cosmopolitan capital. Conference hotels and modern business areas have appeared, and a programme to spruce up the city's façades is ongoing. But despite this, an aura of history and hard times past is evident in the occasional bullet hole from 1956 and flaking 19th-century town house.

Facts + Figures

- Population: 1,700,000
- Size: 525sq km (203sq miles)
- Time: Central European Time (winter: GMT+1; summer: GMT+2)
- Telephone code: 0036 (country), 1 (city)
- Nickname: 'Pearl of the Danube'

BUDAPEST'S FAMOUS

Albert Szent-Györgyi Discovered Vitamin C, which he extracted from paprika.

László Bíró Invented the ballpoint pen after tiring of ink spills.

Ferenc Liszt / Béla Bartók Two of the country's greatest composers.

Ernő Rubik Creator of the famous cube puzzle in the 1980s.

SPA CAPITAL

Landlocked it may be, but Hungary has water in abundance. The earth's crust is relatively thin in this region, and natural thermal water emerges through springs and drilled boreholes. There is a rich bathing tradition. The Romans soaked in Budapest almost 2,000 years ago, and the capital has around 50 baths—more than any other world capital.

NAVIGATION

Finding your way around Budapest is simple. The river splits Pest from Buda. The middle of Pest contains two semi-circular ring roads crossed by straight boulevards radiating outward. The heart of Buda consists of the Castle and Gellért hills rising above the river bank. The city is divided among 23 districts. The middle digits in a postcode indicate the district—thus an address with a postcode of H-1024 is in Buda's District II.

A Short Stay in Budapest

DAY 1

Morning Begin your day at 8.30 with a ride up Castle Hill aboard the Sikló (funicular, ▷ 32). Take an early-morning stroll around the streets of the Castle District before the crowds arrive. Drop in on Mátyás templom (▷ 30) before heading to Bécsi kapu tér and following the outer walls around the northern tip of the district for views over the Buda Hills (▷ 103).

Mid-morning Stop for a cake at Ruszwurm (▷ 36) and then walk to the castle complex at the southern end. There you'll find one of the country's leading collections of national art at the Hungarian National Gallery (▷ 28–29).

Lunch Several of the cafés and restaurants in the Castle District are over-priced. Choose between Café Pierrot (▷ 36) and Rivalda (▷ 36).

Afternoon Leave the Castle District and take a tram from Moszkva tér to the lower station of the Cogwheel Railway. On alighting, either follow one of the trails on foot to János-hegy (▷ 103) or take the Children's Railway there. This hill offers pretty walking routes and a lookout tower. After that, ride the chairlift down the hillside and take bus No. 158 back to Moszkva tér.

Dinner Cross to the Pest side for dinner. If you plan to attend the opera, consider Két szerecsen (▷ 62), Segal (▷ 62), Callas (▷ 61) or a restaurant-bar on Liszt Ferenc tér.

Evening Take in a performance at the splendid State Opera House (▷ 52), spend an evening relaxing over a few drinks on the bustling Liszt Ferenc tér or dance at a club on Hajógyári-sziget.

DAY 2

Morning Start the day by visiting two of Pest's primary landmarks: the Westminster-inspired neo-Gothic **Parliament** building (▷ 54–55) on Kossuth tér and the looming **Szent István Bazilika** (▷ 56–57), home to Hungary's most holy relic.

Mid-morning After that, stroll along the pedestrianized **Váci utca** (▷ 72), the city's main shopping street. Finish off browsing the lace and food at the many stalls of the **Great Market Hall** (▷ 75).

Lunch A good place to stop for a central, filling and well-priced lunch is **Fatál** (▷ 81), just off Váci utca. Alternatively, for something more sleek and funky, try **Mokka** near the Basilica (▷ 62).

Afternoon Take a look around the massive **Hungarian National Museum** (▷ 68) before following the Small Boulevard northward to the start of **Andrássy út** (▷ 86). You can choose either to walk the whole of its two kilometres (1 mile) or take the underground that runs below. The avenue culminates at **Heroes' Square** (▷ 87), containing the **Museum of Fine Arts** (▷ 88–89). Beyond is the lush City Park (▷ 91), where you shouldn't miss the quirky-looking Vajdahunyad Castle (▷ 94). Finish things off with a relaxing soak in the neo-baroque **Széchenyi Baths** (▷ 93).

Dinner If you fancy splashing out, enjoy an elegant dinner at **Gundel** (▷ 98, reserve ahead). Otherwise eat at **Bagolyvár** (▷ 98), its less expensive sister restaurant next door.

Evening Walk along the Pest riverside to enjoy the bridge illuminations, before choosing from the many lively café-bars on Ráday utca.

▶ ▶ ▶

Andrássy út ▷ 86 Elegant boulevard built to emulate Paris's Champs-Élysées.

Aquincum ▷ 102 A rich cluster of archaeological remains from the Roman period.

Budai-hegység ▷ 103 Buda's verdant hills—a pretty backdrop for walks and bike rides.

Városliget ▷ 91 The capital's primary park with a zoo, amusement park, boating lake and castle.

Váci utca ▷ 72 Bustling street of shops and cafés at the heart of the city; this is the tourists' preferred thoroughfare.

Terrorháza ▷ 90 Museum dedicated to the victims of Hungary's Nazi and Communist terror regimes.

Szoborpark ▷ 104 Resting place for Communist statues erected during Soviet rule.

Szépművészeti Múzeum ▷ 88–89 A breathtaking collection of international fine art including Old Masters.

Szent István Bazilika ▷ 56–57 Basilica containing the mummified hand of Hungary's first Christian king.

Országház ▷ 54–55
▲ Majestic Parliament building modelled on that in
▲ London.

Néprajzi Múzeum ▷ 53 Display of traditional costumes and other national folk items.

Nagy Zsinagóga and Zsido Múzeum ▷ 70–71 World's second-largest synagogue, with a museum.

These pages are a quick guide to the Top 25, which are described in more detail later. Here they are listed alphabetically, and the tinted background shows which area they are in.

Budapesti Történeti Múzeum ▷ 24 Collection of historical artefacts in Buda Castle Palace.

Budavári Palota ▷ 26–27 Former royal palace overlooking the Danube from Castle Hill.

Danube Boat Trip ▷ 66 Take a romantic river ride on the Danube by night or by day.

Gellért-hegy ▷ 40 Rugged hill capped with the stocky citadel.

Halászbástya ▷ 25 Turreted monument named after the fishermen who once defended this part of Castle Hill.

Hősök tere ▷ 87 Stately square at the eastern end of Andrássy út.

Hotel Gellért and Gellért gyógyfürdő ▷ 41 Budapest's best-known historic hotel and thermal baths.

Iparművészeti Múzeum ▷ 67 Exhibition of arts and crafts in a stunning art nouveau building.

Magyar Állami Operaház ▷ 52 Extravagant state opera house.

Magyar Nemzeti Galéria ▷ 28–29 Huge collection of Hungarian art dating from the medieval period.

Mátyás templom ▷ 30 Striking Mátyás Church was built during the 1896 millenary celebrations.

Margit-sziget ▷ 42–43 Leafy island lying in the Danube between Margit and Árpád bridges.

Magyar Nemzeti Múzeum ▷ 68–69 The national museum is the country's biggest.

Map labels:
LŐPORTÁRDÚLÓ
Szépművészeti Múzeum
HERMINAMEZŐ
Hősök tere
Városliget
Andrássy út
ISTVÁNMEZŐ
Reiner F park
ERZSÉBÉTVÁROS
Kerepesi temető
OKTOGON TO VÁROSLIGET 83–98
JÓZSEFVÁROS
Iparművészeti Múzeum
KEREPESDÚLÓ
Orczy kert
AROUND BELVÁROS 63–82
Népliget

◀ ◀ ◀

Shopping

Budapest is a modern capital, and there is no shortage of designer boutiques purveying expensive fashion accessories and slick shopping malls hosting many stores over several floors. However, traditional goods are very much to the fore in quaint craftshops, and you'll find interesting and well-priced food in a range of markets. Antiques aren't difficult to find and a glut of bookshops is evidence of the Hungarian cerebral side.

Food

Hungarians are immensely proud of their cuisine. The places to head to buy fresh produce are the indoor and outdoor markets. The most atmospheric are the market halls (vásárcsarnok); several of these date back to the 19th century, the most famous being the Great Market Hall (Nagycsarnok) facing the southern end of Váci utca. Food specialties include sausages and salamis, paprika (a red pepper that is added to many native dishes and is available either whole or ground) and goose liver.

Antiques

The prime area for antiques hunters is Falk Miksa utca in Pest, near Margaret Bridge. This street is lined with antiques shops and galleries selling everything from clocks to fine furniture. Some of the more popular tourist spots (like Váci utca and the Castle District) have stores selling antiques too, but

Window-shopping; salamis and sausages; Váci utca (top to bottom)

BUY THE BOTTLE

Hungary has 22 wine regions and since the fall of Communism the quality has improved steadily with private investment. Look out for bottles of Tokaji Aszú, a white and usually sweet wine that is very well regarded among connoisseurs. Louis XIV famously referred to it as the 'King of Wines, Wine of Kings'. Alternatively, go for a fruit brandy (pálinka) or Unicum, a bitter-tasting herbal liqueur.

be wary of high prices. Elsewhere, you'll find several shops or auction houses operated by a company called BÁV. Be sure to check you are issued with any necessary export permit when buying. There are antiquarian bookshops selling old books, maps and prints opposite the Hungarian National Museum (on Múzeum körút).

Porcelain, Arts and Crafts

The town of Herend, to the north of Lake Balaton, is famous for its fine porcelain—both practical tableware and decorative figurines—and pieces are readily available in antiques stores and dedicated outlets. The other big name in the world of Hungarian ceramics is Zsolnay. The factory in Pécs produces bold and distinctive pieces—indeed, it is responsible for the brightly hued roof tiles adorning some of the city's landmark buildings. Folk centres and the Great Market Hall offer arts and crafts, comprising pottery, lace and wooden toys.

Clothes and Shopping Malls

You'll find Western-style boutiques selling labels that are beyond the reach of most Hungarians in the heart of Pest, and particularly along the tourist-heavy Váci utca. Considerably cheaper clothes shops hug the two Pest ringroads (Kiskörút and Nagykörút). Several shopping malls have sprung up in recent years, the main ones being Mammut, Mom Park and Westend City Center.

A CHRISTMAS CRACKER

If you're there at the right time, it's worth browsing the Christmas Market (running throughout December) in Vörösmarty tér. The square–with its statue of poet Mihály Vörösmarty cocooned in plastic to prevent the marble from cracking in the cold—is filled with dozens of stalls displaying handcrafted items that make excellent gifts. Be sure to fortify yourself with a donut tower (*kürtőskalács*) and a cup of spiced wine!

Shopping by Theme

Whether you're looking for a department store or a quirky boutique, or something in between, you'll find it all in Budapest. On this page shops are listed by theme. For a more detailed write-up, see the individual listings in Budapest by Area.

ANTIQUES AND ART

Belvárosi aukciósház
(▷ 77)
Csók István Galéria (▷ 77)
Várfok galéria (▷ 34)

BOOKS AND MUSIC

Litea (▷ 34)

CHINA AND GLASS

Ajka kristály (▷ 59, 77)
Herendi porcelán (▷ 77)
Zsolnay porcelán (▷ 78)

FASHION

Hugo Boss (▷ 77)
Jackpot and Cottonfield
(▷ 77)
Salamander cipő (▷ 78)
Tisza cipő (▷ 78)

FOOD AND DRINK

Bortársaság (▷ 34)
La Boutique des Vins
(▷ 77)
Első Magyar Borház Rt
(▷ 59)
Magyar Borok Háza
(▷ 34)
Prés Ház Wine Shop and
Museum (▷ 78)
Szamos Marcipán (▷ 78)

GIFTS

Dísz téri piac (▷ 34)
Folkart Centrum (▷ 77)

MARKETS

Christmas Market (▷ 77)
Fény utcai piac (▷ 34)
Lehel Market (▷ 59)
Nagycsarnok (▷ 75, 78)

SHOPPING AREAS

Andrássy út (▷ 59)
Falk Miksa utca (▷ 59)
Mammut (▷ 34)
Szent István tér (▷ 59)
Westend Shopping Center
(▷ 59)

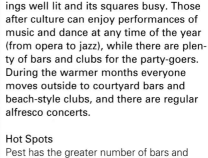

Budapest by Night

Budapest is brilliant by night, its buildings well lit and its squares busy. Those after culture can enjoy performances of music and dance at any time of the year (from opera to jazz), while there are plenty of bars and clubs for the party-goers. During the warmer months everyone moves outside to courtyard bars and beach-style clubs, and there are regular alfresco concerts.

Hot Spots

Pest has the greater number of bars and restaurants. Liszt Ferenc tér—straddling Andrássy út—has traditionally proved a preferred early-evening meeting place. Surrounded with modern café-bars, it fills with people sitting at tables in summer. In recent years, however, an alternative strip has emerged on Ráday utca, right in the heart of the city. This too is lined with a good choice of bars and some feel the service is better and the clientele more down-to-earth. Cafés and bars along the river are frequently attached to hotels and are consequently expensive. Shipyard Island holds several lively nightclubs, which have outdoor venues in summer.

Evening Stroll

When night falls, the promenades running either side of the Danube are obvious places for a romantic walk. Several of the bridges are illuminated, as are riverside monuments like Buda Castle Palace and Parliament.

The illuminated Parliament building at night; Tokaji wine; a popular bar; a candlelit dinner (top to bottom)

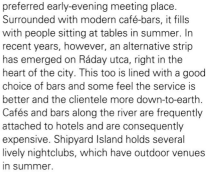

HOT IN THE CITY

In summer, temporary bars and clubs spring up, often occupying disused courtyards or gardens, and changing location from year to year. As such, they can be difficult to find and only become popular through word of mouth. Some of them, however, have been running for a few years—such as West Balkan (behind the Corvin Cinema) and Szimplakert (in the Jewish District).

Eating Out

Hungary's position in Central Europe and its history of occupation by foreign powers means that its cuisine draws on many influences, including German, Austrian, Turkish and Serb. Today there is a wide variety of restaurants to please any taste.

What to Expect

After half a century under communism, Hungary's service industry has taken some time to get back on its feet; now it has, however, it is making giant strides by the year. It remains true though that quality can vary and service can occasionally lack the 'polish' you'd expect in the West. Restaurants in Budapest usually open between midday and around 11pm, but it's safest to arrive before 10pm. With the exception of very exclusive restaurants, there is no formal dress code.

The Choice

The most common word for restaurant is *étterem*, although you might also come across *vendéglő* and *csárda*, the latter specializing in traditional food. As well as Hungarian, many world cuisines are represented. Chinese buffet-style restaurants are popular for quick and inexpensive meals; it's also worth looking out for two- or three-course set 'tourist menus' offered between certain hours of the day. Coffee and cake are ubiquitous in Budapest, and there are some grand cafés. Pâtisseries (*cukrászda*) sell cakes to take away.

TIPPING

It's acceptable to tip 10 per cent in restaurants or to round up a café bill, but always check that service is not included. If you wish to tip, do not leave cash on the table. Instead, indicate the total you wish to pay when the bill is brought to you. If you say 'thank you' as you hand over your money, the staff will assume you don't require any change.

Budapest has many restaurants and cafés where you can eat and drink alfresco

Restaurants by Cuisine

There are restaurants to suit all tastes and budgets in Budapest. On this page they are listed by cuisine. For more a detailed description of each restaurant, see Budapest by Area.

BUDAPEST'S BEST

Belcanto (▷ 80)
Biarritz (▷ 61)
Búsuló Juhász (▷ 48)
Callas (▷ 61)
Gundel (▷ 98)
Mokka (▷ 62)
Pesti Lámpás (▷ 82)
Premier (▷ 98)
Segal (▷ 62)
Spoon–the Boat (▷ 82)

COFFEEHOUSES

Café Pierrot (▷ 36)
Európa kávéház (▷ 62)
Gerbeaud (▷ panel, 82)
Múzeum (▷ 81)
Nagyi palacsintázója (▷ 81)
New York kávéház (▷ 81)
Ruszwurm (▷ 36)

HUNGARIAN

Arany Bárány (▷ 80)
Bagolyvár (▷ 98)
Café Kör (▷ 61)
Fakanál (▷ 81)
Fatál (▷ 81)
Fortuna (▷ 36)
Kárpátia (▷ 81)
Kogart (▷ 98)
Margitkert (▷ 48)
Mátyás pince (▷ 81)
Nádor (▷ 62)
Trófea Grill (▷ 48)

INTERNATIONAL

Apetito (▷ 36)
Arany Kaviár (▷ 36)
Indigo (▷ 98)
Két szerecsen (▷ 62)
Malomtó (▷ 48)
Pata Negra (▷ 82)
Rivalda (▷ 36)
Robinson (▷ 98)
Spinoza Café (▷ 82)

ITALIAN

Magdalena Merlo (▷ 98)
Marxim (▷ 36)
Páva (▷ 62)
Trattoria Pomo d'Oro (▷ 62)
Trattoria Toscana (▷ 82)

SEAFOOD

Admirál (▷ 80)
Baraka (▷ 98)

ESSENTIAL BUDAPEST RESTAURANTS BY CUISINE

If You Like...

However you'd like to spend your time in Budapest, these top suggestions should help you tailor your ideal visit. Each sight or listing has a fuller write-up in Budapest by Area.

CLIMBING HIGH

Ride the funicular (▷ 32) to the Castle District, overlooking the river from the Buda bank.
Take a leg-sapping walk up Gellért Hill (▷ 40) to visit the Citadella (▷ 45) and have a close-up of the Freedom Monument (▷ 46).
Climb up Szent István Bazilika (▷ 56) to the gallery running around the outside of its dome and fabulous city views.

ENTERTAINING THE KIDS

Take them up to the hills on the Children's Railway (▷ 103).
Spend an afternoon at Vidámpark (▷ 94), the permanent funfair in Városliget.
Hit the zoo (▷ 92) and take time yourself to admire the art nouveau elephant house.
Visit the caves (▷ 31) beneath the Castle District.
Get pedalling by hiring a buggy on Margit-sziget (▷ 42).

Riding the funicular (top); the Freedom Monument (above)

TAKING THE WATERS

Soak away your aches in one of the city's many thermal spas, such as Király gyógyfürdő (▷ 45) or Széchenyi gyógyfürdő (▷ 93).
Stroll along the banks the River Danube on the Danube Promenade (▷ 73).
Take a trip to Lake Balaton (▷ 105), the largest lake in Central Europe.
Reserve seats on a romantic river cruise along the Danube (▷ 66), by day or by night.

Enjoying a ride at the funfair (above right); a game of chess in a thermal spa (right)

Váci utca; taking a walk in one of the city's green spaces (below)

WHAT'S FREE

Make a visit to the Hungarian National Museum (▷ 68).
Take a tour of the Parliament building (▷ 54), which is free for those with an EU passport.
Do some window shopping along Váci utca (▷ 72) and soak up the atmosphere in the bustling Nagycsarnok (▷ 75).

NATURE AND GREEN SPACES

Ride the Cogwheel Railway into the Buda Hills (▷ 103), climb the Erzsébet-kilátó (viewing tower) on János-hegy and take the chairlift down the side of the forested hill.
Enjoy the sun with a lazy hour in one of Budapest's leafy parks—Városliget (▷ 91) or Margit-sziget (▷ 42).

HUNGARIAN SPECIALTIES

Browse a market hall for some typical Hungarian produce and a bottle of Bull's Blood (panel, ▷ 59) or Tokaji Aszú (panel, ▷ 10).
Splash out on a meal at the Gundel (▷ 98), a restaurant with a long tradition.
Take a tasting at the House of Hungarian Wines (▷ 34).

Meat shop in a market hall (above); a streetside café (below)

CAFÉ SOCIETY

Find a table at the tiny Ruszwurm (▷ 36), the city's oldest café.
Order a portion of layered cake at the famous Gerbeaud café (▷ panel, 82), named after the Swiss cake maker who managed it in the 1880s.
Take some coffee at the Európa kávéház (▷ 62).

ACCOMMODATION ON A SHOESTRING

Staying in Budapest doesn't have to break the bank

Reserve a private room or apartment through companies like Ibusz or Best Hotel Service (▷ panel, 109).
Sleep in a hostel, such as Marco Polo (▷ 109) or Bánki (▷ 109), or rent a college room during the summer holidays.
Stay in the Castle District on a budget at Kulturinnov (▷ 109).

MUSEUMS AND GALLERIES

Explore the monuments and dark secrets of the country's communist past in the Statue Park (▷ 104) and House of Terror (▷ 90).
Get a taste for Magyar art over the centuries in the Hungarian National Gallery (▷ 28).
Trawl the rich collection of the Hungarian National Museum (▷ 68) and the Roman objects at the Aquincum Museum (▷ 102).

SHOPPING

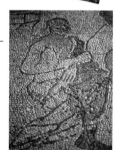

Pick up some traditional craftwork in one of several central shops such as Folkart Centrum on Váci utca (▷ 72).
Buy a piece of fine porcelain from a specialist company outlet like that representing Herend (▷ panel, 77) on József nádor tér.
Taste and purchase Hungarian wine from Bortársaság (▷ 34), the Wine Society with several shops in the city (including that on Batthyány utca).

Statue Park; mosaics at Aquincum (above)

BARS AND CLUBS

Listen to live music at Alcatraz (▷ 79).
Head to Kaktusz Juice for a cocktail or whisky (▷ 97).

Traditional Hungarian products for sale at a market stall (right)

Budapest by Area

Looking down over the river, the Castle District was once the fortified capital of the country and home to the royal court. It has changed face over the centuries, having endured many savage sieges. Today, however, it holds several museums.

5

6

7

8

9

10

D u n a

Moszkva tér

VÉRMEZŐ ÚT

Hattyú utca

Ostrom utca

Batthyány utca

Fiáth J. utca

Várfok utca

Toldy Ferenc utca

Szabó Ilonka utca

Mátray utca

Lovas út

Bécsi Kapu

Levéltár

Kagyló utca

Donáti utca

Babits M. sétány

Toldy Ferenc utca

Franklin utca

Hunfalvy utca

Hadtörténeti Múzeum

Mária Magdolna templom

Kard utca

Országház utca

Tárnok utca

Úri utca

Fortuna utca

M. utca

Tóth Árpád sétány

Lovas út

Logodi utca

Topcsics

Múzeum

Vendéglátóipari Múzeum

Telefónia Múzeum

Szentháromság szobor

Gimnázium utca

Donáti

VÍZIVÁROS

Mátyás templom

Halászbástya

VÁRHEGY

Árpád utca

Régi Budai Városháza

Arany Sas Patika Múzeum

Hunyadi János

Hunyadi

Ponty utca

Fő utca

Iskola utca

Pala utca

Lánchíd utca

KRISZTINAVÁROS

ATTILA ÚT

Vérmező

Déli pályaudvar

DÉLI PÁLYAUDVAR

ALKOTÁS UTCA

Logodi utca

Bugát utca

Budavári Labirintus

Szent György utca

Dísz tér

Szent György utca

Színház utca

Várszínház

Clark Ádám tér

Sikló

Kosciuszkó utca

Krisztina körút

Miko utca

Pauler utca

Palota utca

ALAGÚT UTCA

Legújabbkori Tört Múzeum

Szinyei M. utca

Savoyai Jenő szobor

Magyar Nemzeti Galéria

Festetics utca

Kuny Domokos utca

MÉSZÁROS UTCA

Horváth-kert

Váralja

Budavári Palota

Budapesti Történeti Múzeum

ATTILA ÚT

Országos Széchenyi Könyvtár

Ag utca

Gellérthegy utca

Tigris utca

Fenyő utca

Nap hegy

Orvos utca

Úsznál utca

NAPHEGY

Krisztina körút

A   **B**

0 ——— 250 m

0 ——— 250 yds

Duna

C D E

Budapesti Történeti Múzeum

A 14th-century statue of a courtier on display in the Knights' Hall (right)

THE BASICS

www.btm.hu

➕ B8

✉ I, Szent György tér 2

☎ 487 8800

🕐 1 Mar–15 May, 16 Sep–31 Oct Tue–Sun 10–6; 16 May–15 Sep daily 10–6; 1 Nov–28 Feb Tue–Sun 10–4

🚌 Bus: 5, 16, 78; tram: 18; Sikló (funicular)

♿ Good (except no access to Knights' Hall and King's Cellar)

💵 Moderate

❓ Guided tours available

HIGHLIGHTS

● Gold finds from Avar burial mounds

● Capture of King Porus by József Szentpéteri—a silver piece shown at London's Great Exhibition of 1851

● Red-marble door frame adorned with a raven—the seal of King Mátyás

The Budapest History Museum offers a rare glimpse of the medieval palace lying deep beneath the current complex. These remains were uncovered during renovations and excavations following the savage bombardment of the Castle District at the end of World War II.

History of the city The floors above ground are dedicated to exhibits charting the city's history from the prehistoric age up to the 1990s. There are finds left by the various tribes who ruled the region in the centuries before the arrival of the Magyars—ancestors of today's Hungarians—and a well-crafted chronological portrayal of the birth and growth of 'modern' Budapest. The latter takes 1686 as its starting point, the year that Buda was 'liberated' from Turkish rule by the Habsburgs, moves through the Great Flood of 1838 and millennial celebrations of 1896, and culminates in the decade that followed the end of Communism.

Down below Accessed via a basement below the museum are the scant remains of what was the medieval palace. The palace reached its zenith during the 15th-century rule of King Mátyás, whose court was one of Europe's Renaissance powerhouses. The Renaissance Hall contains objects dating from that period. The 14th-century statues of contemporary courtiers displayed in the Knights' Hall are valuable because few statues of this kind survived the Ottoman occupation.

Halászbástya

Despite its medieval styling, the Fishermen's Bastion—so called because this was supposedly the area of the Castle District defended by members of the Guild of Fishermen—is actually little more than a century old.

Fishermen's Bastion The Fishermen's Bastion is the work of Frigyes Schulek, who added it in 1902 to complement the adjacent Mátyás Church (which he also designed). Unlike the painstakingly researched statue in front of it (▷ below), the formidable looking neo-Romanesque structure is a pure work of fantasy and bears little relation to genuine medieval fortifications. The turrets represent the seven Magyar tribes that settled in Hungary at the end of the first millennium. These were nomadic people, reflected in the deliberately tent-like appearance of the bastion's turrets. The bastion has upper and lower levels affording good views over Pest across the river.

St. István statue Schulek's fanciful flight continues on the plinth of the bronze equestrian statue of King István, which stands in front of the bastion. King István was responsible for suppressing the country's pagan factions and introducing Christianity. On a relief at the rear of the plinth, the bearded architect imagines himself presenting the church to István. The statue itself was the work of Alajos Stróbl, who took a decade researching 11th-century riding garb and armour in his quest for medieval authenticity.

THE BASICS

➕ B7
✉ I, Szentháromság tér
🚌 Bus: 16, Várbusz
♿ Lower terrace good, upper terrace none
🎫 Upper terrace
15 Mar–15 Oct daily
9am–11pm: inexpensive;
rest of year: free

HIGHLIGHTS

● The fierce-looking, helmeted statues depicting the Magyar tribal leaders
● Views over the river

TIP

● Don't bother paying to reach the upper terrace in high season—the views are very nearly as good from the lower level, and equally good from the area in front of Buda Castle Palace (which is free to enter).

CASTLE DISTRICT

TOP 25

Budavári Palota

TOP 25

HIGHLIGHTS

● The bronze *turul*—a mythical bird said to have fathered Árpád's own father, and thus an ancestor of the Magyars—at the first entrance to the palace complex
● The Mátyás Well in a courtyard at the back of the palace

TIPS

● Head to the terrace at the front of the palace for some exquisite views of the city.
● You can take a lift up to the complex from Dózsa György tér.

Buda Castle Palace looms high over the river and is one of the city's enduring symbols. The royal residence for centuries, today it houses two of Budapest's main museums.

The early days Castle Hill first became a royal complex under Béla IV in the 13th century. Returning from exile to a country decimated by the Mongol invasion of 1241–42, he recognized the hill's defensive advantages and constructed a town on top with a castle and fortified walls. Later monarchs built their palaces at the southern end of the hill, the most impressive being that of King Mátyás Corvinus. Mátyás was one of Europe's great 15th-century kings, and his court a hub of Renaissance culture and thinking. There are a few remains of his palace (as

Buda Castle Palace, on the riverside, now contains the Hungarian National Gallery and the Budapest History Museum

well as that of the earlier Gothic palace of King Zsigmond) in the Budapest History Museum.

More recent history The building was destroyed during the battle to eject the Turks in 1686, after which the Habsburgs constructed a palace in its place. Expansion after the Austro-Hungarian Compromise of 1867, under the renowned architects Miklós Ybl and Alajos Hauszmann, included lengthening the façade and adding a dome. During World War II, the Russians besieged the hill where the German army had retreated in a vain attempt to hold the city. Fighting was fierce and the palace was severely damaged once more. The reconstruction was heavily tailored to 20th-century tastes. The simple, neoclassical version of the dome is typical of this shift.

THE BASICS

✚ B8
✉ I, Szent György tér 2
☎ 1 224 3700
🌐 Only the museums (National Gallery, History Museum) and Széchenyi Library are open to the public
🚌 Bus: 5, 16, 78; tram: 18; Sikló (funicular railway)
♿ Mainly good (lift access to most—though not all—areas of museums and library)

27

HIGHLIGHTS

● *The Visitation* (1506) by the anonymous 'Master MS' (first floor, Wing D)
● *Thunderstorm over the Puszta* (1853) by Károly Lotz (first floor, Wing C)
● *Condemned Cell I* (1870) by Mihály Munkácsy (first floor, Wing B)
● *Pilgrimage to the Cedars of Lebanon* (1907) by Tivadar Csontváry Kosztka (second floor, Wing C)

TIP

● Book in advance for a guided tour—given the museum's size, it's well worth it to ensure you get straight to the good (and bypass the bad).

Spreading across three wings of the Buda Castle Palace, the Hungarian National Gallery holds 100,000 works and is the country's biggest and best collection of Hungarian art.

Early art The gallery was spawned during the 19th-century reform movement captured by the irrepressibly energetic Count István Széchenyi, and displays works dating from the 10th century up to the modern era. It opens on the ground floor of Wing D with the Medieval and Renaissance Lapidarium, showcasing some church art and architectural pieces including painted panels and Gothic altarpieces from the 15th century. Also here are carved details from the palace of King Mátyás. Directly above on the first floor is a display of beautiful late-

Visitors looking at a portrait; a statue from the Middle Ages; a baroque painting; Hungarian coronation regalia, including a jewelled crown; Hungarian royal seals (clockwise from left)

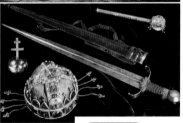

Gothic winged altars and some late-Renaissance and baroque works (many of them once owned by the Eszterházy family).

19th- and 20th-century art Art from the 19th century occupies the rest of the first floor in Wings B and C. Keep an eye out for great names of the period like Károly Lotz, famous for his moody Romanticist landscape depictions of life on the *puszta*, and Mihály Munkácsy, whose late 19th-century works were often infused with powerful and sombre social messages. The next floor is devoted to 20th-century artists. You won't miss the massive canvases by Tivadar Csontváry Kosztka, and other highlights include portraits by József Rippl-Rónai, plein-air pieces by József Egry and expressionist works by Vilmos Aba-Novák.

THE BASICS

www.mng.hu
➕ B8
✉ I, Szent György tér 2
☎ 1 201 9082
🕐 Tue–Sun 10–6
🍴 Café
🚌 Bus: 5, 16, 78; tram: 18; Sikló (funicular)
♿ Good (access via Wing A)
🎫 Permanent exhibitions: free; temporary exhibitions: moderate; access to the dome: inexpensive
❓ Guided tour available

Mátyás templom

Beautiful roof tiles adorn Mátyás Church (left and right)

THE BASICS

www.matyas-templom.hu
⊞ B7
✉ I, Szentháromság tér 2
☎ 1 355 5657
🕐 Mon–Fri 9–5, Sat 9–12, Sun 1–5
🚌 Bus: 16; Várbusz
♿ Mainly good (access via visitors' exit)
💶 Moderate
❓ Audio guide available in numerous languages

HIGHLIGHTS

● The 14th-century Maria portal, at the southern side of the church. The relief above it shows the assumption of the Virgin Mary
● Copies of the Hungarian Holy Crown up some stairs in the royal oratory

Located in the heart of the Castle District, its spire a prominent feature of the Buda riverscape, the Mátyás Church is awash with colour—from its roof tiles to the painted stone walls inside.

The background Mátyás Church—officially called the Church of Our Lady—was first constructed between 1255 and 1269 for Buda's German population, and a few scraps of masonry and stone carvings remain in the current incarnation. It underwent several reconstructions over the centuries and was used as a mosque by the Turks and for the coronation of Ferenc József in 1867. The main overhaul was commissioned at the close of the 19th century to celebrate the 1,000-year anniversary of the Magyar arrival. The architect Frigyes Schulek undertook meticulous research in his quest to revive the Gothic spirit of the original. Later it was used as a kitchen by German soldiers during World War II, then as a Soviet stable, before being restored in 1970.

Inside the church The interior is painted with patterns based on patches of surviving decoration from the Middle Ages. The frescoes showing famous moments in Hungary's history are by historicist artists Károly Lotz and Bertalan Székely. The Béla Chapel on the northern side of the church contains the remains of the 12th-century King Béla III, while the St László Chapel has a replica of the beautiful gold bust of László (the real one is held in Győr Cathedral).

More to See

ARANY SAS PATIKA MÚZEUM

The Golden Eagle Pharmacy Museum contains furnishings and medical items from Buda's first pharmacy, opened in the 17th century. There's also a display of the often stomach-turning ingredients to be found in an alchemist's lab.

🚩 B7 ✉ I, Tárnok utca 18 ☎ 1 375 9772 🕐 Nov to mid-Mar Tue–Thu 10.30–3.30, Fri–Sun 10.30–5.30; mid-Mar to Oct Tue–Sun 10.30–5.30 🚌 Bus: 16, Várbusz ♿ Good inside; one step outside entrance 💷 Free

BÉCSI KAPU

Vienna Gate leads into the northern end of the Castle District. The original medieval gate was destroyed during the siege to expel the Turks in 1686, and the one you see today was constructed between the wars. The square's main sights include a late 19th-century Lutheran church, the National Archives and the Museum of Military History (▷ opposite). You can also reach the outer walls from here, which offer views over the Buda Hills.

🚩 A7 🚇 Moszkva tér 🚌 Bus: 16, Várbusz

BUDAVÁRI LABIRINTUS

www.labirintus.com

The cave system below the Castle District was used as a military installation during the communist period. Now the chambers are filled with waxworks evoking important events in Hungary's history.

🚩 B8 ✉ I, Úri utca 9 ☎ 1 212 0207 🕐 Daily 9.30–7.30 🚌 Bus: 16, Várbusz ♿ Access via Lovas út entrance (outside Castle District walls) 💷 Moderate

HADTÖRTÉNETI MÚZEUM

www.militaria.hu

The Museum of Military History—whose entrance is on Tóth Árpád sétány, behind Bécsi kapu tér—is in a late 19th-century barracks building and has exhibitions on the Hungarian Hussar regiment, the 1848–49 Independence War and the World Wars.

🚩 A7 ✉ I, Tóth Árpád sétány 40 ☎ 1 325 1600 🕐 Apr–Sep Tue–Sun 10–6,

Entrance to the Buda Castle Labyrinth

Statue at Bécsi Kapu (Vienna Gate)

Oct–Mar Tue–Sun 10–4 (closed 24–26 Dec, 1–7 Jan) 🚇 Moszkva tér 🚌 Bus: 16, Várbusz ♿ Good 🎟️ Free

MÁRIA MAGDOLNA TEMPLOM

The bulk of the Church of Mary Magdalene was destroyed during bombing in 1944, but the tower was preserved. The 13th-century church was constructed for Hungarian residents (German settlers used the Mátyás Church). ✚ A7 ✉️ I, Kapisztrán tér 6 🚇 Moszkva tér 🚌 Bus: 16, Várbusz

ORSZÁGOS SZÉCHÉNYI KÖNYVTÁR

www.oszk.hu

The National Széchényi Library, which is now situated in the palace, was founded in 1802 by Ferenc Széchényi (father of the great reformer, István). He dreamed of making Hungary one of Europe's powerhouses of learning. There are a few corvina codices from King Mátyás's lauded Renaissance library.

✚ B8 ✉️ I, Wing F, Budavári palota ☎️ 1 224 3742 🕐 Reading rooms: Tue–Fri 9–9, Sat 10–8; closed Aug. Foreign-language tours (by appointment) 🍴 Café 🚌 Bus: 16, Várbusz ♿ Good 🎟️ Inexpensive

RÉGI BUDAI VÁROSHÁZA

The former Buda town hall was built in the late 17th century before the unification of the three settlements (Buda, Pest and Óbuda) to form a single city. There's a statue of Pallas Athene, the Guardian of Buda, at the corner of the building. ✚ B7 ✉️ Szentháromság tér 2 🚌 Bus: 16, Várbusz

SIKLÓ

If you don't fancy climbing the sloping walkways leading up Castle Hill, take the funicular railway. Originally built in 1870, it had to be rebuilt after damage during World War II. ✚ B8 ✉️ I, Clark Ádám tér–Szent György tér ☎️ 1 461 6688 🕐 Daily 7.30–10; closed 2–6 Apr, every second Mon of the month 🚌 Bus: 4, 16, 86, 105; tram: 19, 41 ♿ Good 🎟️ Moderate

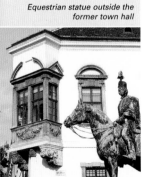

Sikló (funicular railway)

Equestrian statue outside the former town hall

Castle Walk

Take in the main sights of the Castle District and enjoy views over the Buda Hills from its fortified walls.

DISTANCE: 1.5km (1 mile) **ALLOW:** 1–1.5 hours

START

SZENT GYÖRGY TÉR
➕ B8 🚠 Sikló (funicular)

END

DÍSZ TÉR ➕ B8 🚌 Bus: 16, Várbusz; Sikló from Szent György tér

❶ Take the funicular (▷ 32) from Clark Ádám tér to Szent György tér. Sándor Palace, the president's official residence, is on the right as you alight.

❽ Then head to the right along Úri utca past the Buda Castle Labyrinth (▷ 31). Finish at Dísz tér.

❷ Turn left and pass through the first gate into the palace complex (▷ 26), following the steps down to the river-facing terrace at the front. Turn right through the arch behind the statue of Eugene of Savoy.

❼ Follow the promenade running along the district's outer wall, past a memorial to the last Turkish governor. Tóth Árpád sétány is home to the Museum of Military History (▷ 31). Turn left on to Szentháromság utca, stopping at the Ruszwurm (▷ 36).

❸ Take a look at the Mátyás Well, turn left into the Lion Courtyard and then return to Szent György tér by the second gate (past the statue of the horseherd). Follow Szent György utca to Dísz tér.

❻ Move left into the adjoining Kapisztrán tér, home to the single tower of the Church of Mary Magdalene (▷ 32), and then climb some steps to the right of the National Archives.

❹ Walk up Tárnok utca, past the Golden Eagle Pharmacy Museum (▷ 31) and on to Szentháromság tér. See Mátyás Church (▷ 30) and the Fishermen's Bastion (▷ 25).

❺ Continue up Táncsics Mihály utca until you reach Bécsi kapu tér.

Shopping

BORTÁRSASÁG

www.bortarsasag.hu
One of several shops
operated by the
Hungarian Wine Society,
this store offers free
wine-tasting sessions
on Saturday afternoons
and has a wide range
of wines from all over
the country.
➕ B6 ✉ I, Batthyány utca
59 ☎ 212 2569
🕐 Mon–Fri 10–8, Sat 10–6
🚌 Bus: 11, 39

DÍSZ TÉRI PIAC

This daily outdoor
market on the eastern
side of Dísz tér sells
handicrafts, embroidery
and other traditional
goods likely to appeal to
the many tourists who
visit the Castle District.
➕ B8 ✉ I, Dísz tér
🕐 Daily 10–6 🚌 Bus: 16,
Várbusz

FÉNY UTCAI PIAC

Situated behind
Mammut (▷ this page),
just off Moszkva tér,
this vibrant market sells
an array of meat,
vegetables, cheeses,
wines, flowers and
pickles. The stalls are
outside, but are protect-
ed from the elements
by a transparent roof.
➕ A6 ✉ II, Lövőház utca 12
☎ 1 345 4101 🕐 Mon–Fri
6–6, Sat 6–2 🚇 Moszkva
tér

LITEA

www.litea.hu
This diminutive shop on
a back alley off Hess
András tér sells books
and CDs, and also has
tables where you can
enjoy a hot drink. You'll
find the entrance to the
alley on the opposite
side of the road from
the Hilton.
➕ B7 ✉ I, Hess András tér
4 ☎ 1 375 6987 🕐 Daily
10–6 🚌 Bus: Várbusz

MAGYAR BOROK HÁZA

www.winehouse.hu
The House of Hungarian
Wines stands opposite
the Hilton, and offers
wines from all the
country's 22 regions. It
has a large cellar with
sections devoted to the
different wine areas.
You can also take a
two-hour tasting
session in the cellar,
during which you can
sample as many of the
selected wines as you

> ### SHOPPING IN THE CASTLE DISTRICT
>
> Most of the best shopping
> districts are on the Pest
> side of the river. The
> Castle District has little
> shops selling glass,
> antiques, art and leather
> goods. Be wary, however,
> because prices can be
> expensive in what is one
> of the city's main tourist
> areas.

like for a fixed price.
➕ B7 ✉ I, Szentháromság
tér 6 ☎ 1 212 1031
🕐 Daily 12–8 🚌 Bus:
Várbusz

MAMMUT

www.mammut.hu
Divided between two
enormous buildings
either side of Lövőház
utca, at the back of
Széna tér (next to
Moszkva tér), Mammut
is one of the city's
leading shopping malls.
As well as over 300
shops offering books,
clothes, jewellery and
electrical goods, there
are bars, nightclubs, a
cinema complex and a
fitness area. It's a
popular place with the
city's youth.
➕ A6 ✉ II, Lövőház utca
2–6 ☎ 1 345 8020 🕐 Daily
10–7 🚇 Moszkva tér

VÁRFOK GALÉRIA

Works of Hungarian art
are sold from this
gallery, which is a short
walk from Bécsi kapu
(▷ 31) to the north of
the Castle District.
➕ A7 ✉ I, Várfok utca 14
☎ 1 213 5155 🕐 Tue–Sat
11–6 🚇 Moszkva tér

Entertainment and Nightlife

CAFÉ MIRÓ

This café-bar is well positioned near Mátyás Church (▷ 30), and displays the works of artist Joan Miró. It has a funky atmosphere, playing contemporary music amid modern furnishings.

➕ A7 ✉ I, Úri utca 30 ☎ 1 201 5573 🕐 Daily 9–midnight 🚌 Bus: Várbusz

JAM PUB

www.jampub.hu
There are several bars and clubs in the Mammut shopping mall (▷ 34). Jam is one of these, situated on the ground floor.

➕ A6 ✉ II, Mammut II, Lövőház utca 2–6 🕐 Sun–Wed 9–2, Thu–Sat 9–4 🚇 Moszkva tér

MANNA

www.mannalounge.com
Manna—a bar and restaurant playing live music in the evening—sits above the western side of the tunnel that runs through Castle Hill. There are also large video installations showing European urban scenes.

➕ B8 ✉ II, Palota út 17 ☎ 20 9999 188 🕐 Daily 6–1 🚌 Bus: 5

MILLENÁRIS PARK

www.millenaris.hu
This cultural and recreational area in a purpose-built park behind Moszkva tér has concerts and festivals.

There are two indoor performance spaces and in the warmer months events are hosted outside.

➕ A6 ✉ II, Fény utca 20–22 🚇 Moszkva tér

NEMZETI TÁNCSZÍNHÁZ

www.dancetheatre.hu
The National Dance Theatre, next to the Sándor Palace, stages performances of classical and modern dance. It is based on the site of a former monastery but functioned as a theatre from the late 1700s, when the religious orders were banned. In addition to the two indoor arenas, alfresco shows are performed in

---

NATIONAL DANCE THEATRE

The National Dance Theatre was founded in the 18th century in a former monastery building that had become redundant when József II disbanded the order. Like the Mátyás Church, it catered primarily to the significant German population that lived in the Castle District. Despite this, in 1790 it hosted the first-ever professional play performed in the Hungarian language. Its other claim to fame is that Beethoven played inside in 1800.

---

the Carmelite courtyard in the summer.

➕ B8 ✉ I, Színház utca 1–3 ☎ 1 356 4085 🚌 Bus: 16, Várbusz

OSCAR BAR

Basement bar a short distance outside Bécsi kapu that is devoted to the old world of Hollywood film.

➕ A7 ✉ I, Ostrom utca 14 ☎ 1 212 8017 🕐 Sun–Thu 5–2, Fri–Sat 5–4 🚇 Moszkva tér

VÁRKERT CASINO

www.varkert.com
Standing below the southern end of Castle Hill, on the Buda river bank, this casino is housed in an elegant old pump house and stays open until well into the early hours. Photo ID is required for entry. The dress code is smart-casual, so you will be refused admittance if you are in shorts or scruffy-looking clothes.

➕ C9 ✉ I, Ybl Miklós tér 9 ☎ 1 202 4244 🕐 Daily 11am–6am 🚋 Tram: 19, 41

Restaurants

PRICES

Prices are approximate, based on a 3-course meal for one person.
€€€   over 5,000Ft
€€   3,000–5,000Ft
€   under 3,000Ft

APETITO (€€)
www.apetito.hu
Innovative restaurant where you choose a selection of appetizer portions of the dishes on the menu. It can be found near Mátyás Church (▷ 30).
➕ B7 ✉ I, Hess András tér 6 ☎ 1 488 7416 ⏰ Daily 11am–midnight 🚌 Bus: Várbusz

ARANY KAVIÁR (€€€)
www.aranykaviar.hu
Good, intimate restaurant on the road below Bécsi kapu (▷ 31) specializing in Russian cuisine and that of other former Soviet states like Ukraine and Georgia. You can order iced glasses of vodka and there is a selection of dishes featruring caviar. The fin-de-siècle decor creates an elegant ambience.
➕ A7 ✉ I, Ostrom utca 19 ☎ 1 201 6737 ⏰ Daily 12–12 🚇 Moszkva tér 🚌 Bus: 39, Várbusz

CAFÉ PIERROT (€€)
Well-regarded café and restaurant toward the northern end of the Castle District. It has been running for over a quarter of a century and remains one of the leading places to dine in the area.
➕ A7 ✉ I, Fortuna utca 14 ☎ 1 375 6971 ⏰ Daily 11am–midnight 🚌 Bus: Várbusz

FORTUNA (€€€)
www.fortuna-restaurant.hu
The Fortuna House was once the site of the press that printed the first book in Hungarian in 1443. The current building dates to the early 20th century. The restaurant contains several rooms with knightly themes, and there is also a cellar area where you have the opportunity to bottle and label your own sparkling wine. Some famous figures

CAFÉ CULTURE

While the Ruszwurm is the city's longest-established café, it is far from the only one with a distinguished history. The café or coffeehouse played a vital social role in the 19th and early 20th centuries as a meeting place and social forum (often for artists and political thinkers). Many were lavishly furnished, and some remain in the city centre today including Gerbeaud, the Centrál and the New York.

have signed bottles in storage here.
➕ A7 ✉ I, Hess András tér 4 ☎ 1 375 6857 ⏰ Daily 11–11 🚌 Bus: Várbusz

MARXIM (€)
This is a fun pizzeria with a Communist theme. Pizzas have Soviet-related names and you sit in divided booths. The food is excellent value.
➕ A6 ✉ II, Kis Rókus utca 23 ☎ 1 316 0231 ⏰ Mon–Thu noon–1am, Fri–Sat noon–2am, Sun 6pm–1am 🚇 Moszkva tér 🚋 Tram: 4, 6

RIVALDA (€€)
www.rivalda.net
Restaurant with a theatrical theme next to the National Dance Theatre (panel, ▷ 35). In summer you can eat in the former monastery courtyard.
➕ B8 ✉ I, Színház utca 5–9 ☎ 1 489 0236 ⏰ Daily 11.30–11.30 🚌 Bus: 16, Várbusz

RUSZWURM (€€)
www.ruszwurm.hu
Ruszwurm is the oldest café (and one of the smallest) in the city, established in 1827, and decorated with lovely Biedermeier furnishings. This was a favourite place of Empress Sissi.
➕ A7 ✉ I, Szentháromság utca 7 ☎ 1 375 5284 ⏰ Daily 10–7 🚌 Bus: Várbusz

Gellért Hill rises to the south of Castle Hill, crowned with the Citadella and Freedom Monument. Serb immigrants settled in the area between the two hills—known as the Tabán—during the 18th century. Residential streets lead up Rose Hill to the north.

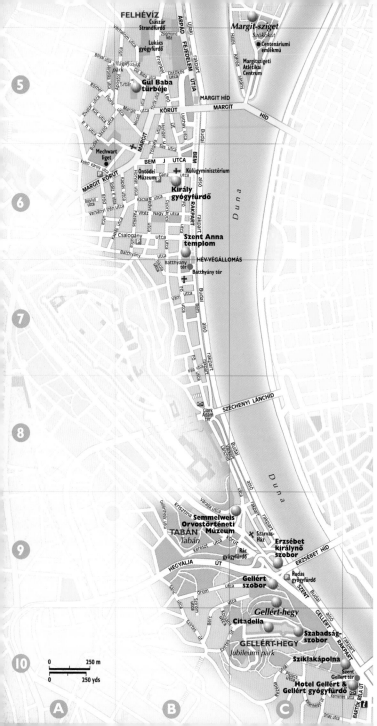

SZABADSÁG HID

Gellért-hegy

Stunning view of Pest and the Danube (left); Gellért Statue (right)

THE BASICS

➕ C9

🍴 Restaurant just below the citadel on Szirtes út

🚌 Bus: 27 (up the hill); bus: 7, red 7, 7A, 8, 27, 86, red 173; tram 18, 19, 47, 49 (to the base of the hill)

♿ Ascent difficult without transport

🎫 Free

HIGHLIGHTS

● Cave Chapel (▷ 46)
● Citadel (▷ 45)
● Freedom Monument—a statue of a woman holding a palm leaf above her head (▷ 46)
● Gellért Statue (▷ 45)
● The river views

If you fancy a bit of exercise, brave a tramp up Gellért Hill. At its pinnacle are a couple of the city's most recognizable landmarks—and you can take a bird's eye view of the river below.

The name The 140m (459ft) granite hill is named after an Italian bishop who was martyred here in the 11th century. When King István decided to adopt Christianity as the state religion—in part as a means of unifying the country and dispatching rivals—he employed the services of the missionary bishop Gellért. When István died heirless, there was a power vacuum during which the unfortunate bishop was nailed inside a barrel and thrown down the hill by pagans. A statue of him (▷ 45) bearing a crucifix stands part way up the hill, directly above Elizabeth Bridge.

Getting to the top There are several ways to scale the hill's heights. There is a car park, and the No. 27 bus will carry you most of the way (catch it from Móricz Zsigmond körtér). However, if you can stand the tough walk up then you'll get the most from what the hill has to offer. Paths snake their way up its sides, and there are benches and viewing points along the way. If you start from opposite the Hotel Gellért (▷ 41), visit the Cave Chapel (▷ 46) before continuing up to the top. Once there, you can walk around the citadel (▷ 45) —built by the Habsburgs to counter further rebellion after the 1848–49 Independence War.

Hotel Gellért (right) and its famous baths (left)

Hotel Gel...
Gellért gyó...

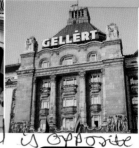

cave chapel is opposite

Built in the early 20th century, the Hotel Gellért is probably the city's best-known place to stay. The opulent baths next door are fed by thermal springs bubbling up from deep beneath Gellért Hill.

The hotel Bishop Gellért is well remembered on the Buda side of Freedom Bridge, where Gellért Hill faces the Hotel Gellért and the Gellért Baths across Gellért tér. The art-nouveau hotel ranks among Budapest's leading historic accommodation hot spots, having been completed in 1918. Its broad, symmetrical façade looks lovely when illuminated at night and there is a porcelain fountain in front. Guests can enter the adjacent baths free of charge.

The baths The impressive Gellért Baths are the most popular with tourists—and are consequently the city's costliest. The entrance hall is adorned with bright tiles from the Zsolnay factory in Pécs and stained-glass windows depicting episodes from an epic Hungarian poem. There is a mixed pool, as well as separate thermal baths for men and women, and an outdoor area for sunbathing (around a large pool with wave machine).

On entering you buy a ticket either for a private changing cubicle or a locker in a shared area. If you choose the latter, you'll be given a tag with a number on it. Take the tag to the changing room attendant, who will open a locker for you and chalk your tag number on the inside of the door; remember your locker number.

THE BASICS

www.danubiushotels.com
🔲 D10
✉ XI, Szent Gellért tér 1
☎ 889 5500 (hotel);
466 6166 (baths)
🕐 Baths: high season daily 6am–7pm (also 13 Jun–16 Aug Fri–Sat 8pm–midnight); low season Mon–Fri 6am–7pm, Sat–Sun 6–5
🍴 Restaurants, café, bar
🚌 Bus: 7, red 7, 7A, 8, 27, 86, red 173; tram: 18, 19, 47, 49
♿ Poor but baths are being renovated and will offer easier access
💷 Baths: expensive; less expensive after 4pm

HIGHLIGHT

● The wave machine in the outdoor pool

TIP

● You can refund part of your entrance fee if you stay fewer than 4 hours.

Margit-sziget

HIGHLIGHT

● Exploring the island on a *bringóhintó*—a pedal-powered buggy available to hire near the southern end

TIP

● Cars may access the island from Árpád Bridge (as far as a car park at the northern end). Only bus No. 26 runs on to the island itself.

Margaret Island—topped and tailed by the Árpád and Margit bridges—is a summer favourite with Budapest residents, who come here to swim, cycle, stroll or just laze about on the grass while enjoying the sun.

The history Known as the Island of Hares in Roman times, Margaret Island may then have been a retreat for lepers (the Latin words for hare and leper being similar). Later it was the site of a Turkish pasha's harem and enjoyed a soft spot in the heart of Palatine Ferenc I, who planted rare trees during the late 18th century. The current name is a reminder of its more sober history as a hub of monasticism; following the Mongol invasion of 1241–42, King Béla IV promised his next-born would spend a life of

A water tower overlooks one of Margaret Island's green spaces (left); jogging by the river (middle); the Japanese garden (right)

religious devotion in return for God's future protection of Hungary. He was true to his word, and his famously pious daughter Margit lived on the island. Writers and artists flocked here during the 19th century to take advantage of the medicinal waters in a bathing hall designed by architect Miklós Ybl.

The sights You can walk on to the island from Margaret Bridge. Heading north you'll pass the Palatinus Swimming Baths, which boast several pools and water slides. There are remains of a medieval Franciscan church to the east of the baths, while farther up are the foundations of the Dominican church and cloister built for Margit. The rebuilt Premonstratensian chapel originally dated to the 11th–12th centuries and is the city's earliest structure.

More to See

CITADELLA
www.citadella.hu
The citadel at the top of Gellért Hill was built by the Habsburgs after the failed uprising against their rule in 1848–49 as a deterrent to future rebellion. Today there is an exhibition covering the history of the hill inside its walls.

➕ C10 🍴 Restaurant and café facilities 🚍 Bus: 27 ♿ Good (approach from back of the hill) 💷 Inexpensive (access to the exhibition)

ERZSÉBET KIRÁLYNŐ SZOBOR
A bronze statue of the popular 19th-century Empress Erzsébet—known as Sissi—sits just to the north of Elizabeth Bridge.

➕ C9 ✉ I, Döbrentei tér 🚍 Bus: 5, 7, 8, 78, 86, 112, 173; tram: 18, 19, 41, 118

GELLÉRT SZOBOR
A staggered path behind Elizabeth Bridge leads up to a waterfall and statue of Gellért. The bishop was right-hand man of King István and tutor to his son, and was gruesomely murdered here by pagans in 1046 after the king's death.

➕ C9 ✉ XI, Gellért-hegy 🚍 Bus: 5, 7, 8, 27, 78, 86, 112, 173; tram: 18, 19, 41, 118

GÜL BABA TÜRBÉJE
At the top of Rózsadomb is the 16th-century tomb of Gül Baba, a Turkish dervish who lived on the hill. He is said to have grown flowers and became known as the 'Father of Roses'.

➕ B5 ✉ II, Mecset utca 14 ☎ 326 0062 🕐 Jan–Apr daily 10–6, May–Sep Tue–Sun 10–6, Oct Tue–Sun 10–5, Nov–Feb daily 10–4 🍴 Café next door 🚍 Bus: 191; tram: 4, 6, 17 ♿ None (and there are several sets of stairs, which makes access difficult) 💷 Inexpensive

KIRÁLY GYÓGYFÜRDŐ
The 16th-century Király (King) Baths have an original Turkish cupola, and are open to men and women on different days.

➕ B6 ✉ II, Fő utca 84 ☎ 202 3688 🕐 Women: Tue, Thu 6.30am–7pm, Sat

Bronze statue of Empress Erzsébet (above)

Freedom Monument (opposite)

Tomb of Gül Baba (right)

6.30am–1pm; men: Mon, Wed, Fri 9–9 (closed Sun) 🚌 Bus 60, 86; tram: 19, 41 ♿ None ✋ Moderate

SEMMELWEIS ORVOSTÖRTÉNETI MÚZEUM

www.semmelweis.museum.hu
Ignác Semmelweis was a Hungarian doctor who discovered the link between deaths in childbirth and poor hospital hygiene. The house where he was born contains a history of medicine.

✚ C9 ✉ I, Apród utca 1–3 ☎ 375 3533 🕐 Mar–Oct Tue–Sun 10.30–6, Nov–Feb Tue–Sun 10.30–4 (closed Easter, Christmas, 20 Aug) 🚌 Bus: 5, 78, 86; tram 19, 41 ♿ None (museum is upstairs on the first floor) ✋ Free (permanent exhibitions), inexpensive (temporary exhibitions)

SZABADSÁG-SZOBOR

The Freedom Monument was originally created for Admiral Horthy as a tribute to his son (who died during World War II). When the Russians 'liberated' the city, however, they placed the palm of victory in the hands of the female figure, and it became a taunting symbol of Communist oppression.

✚ C10 ✉ XI, Gellért-hegy 🚌 Bus: 27

SZENT ANNA TEMPLOM

The baroque St. Anna Church was commissioned by the Jesuits in 1740, but circumstances—including the dissolution of the Jesuit order—meant it wasn't consecrated for another 65 years.

✚ B6 ✉ I, Batthyány tér 7 ☎ 201 3404 🚇 Batthyány tér 🚌 Bus: 11, 39, 60, 86; tram 19, 41 ♿ None ❓ Regular concerts

SZIKLAKÁPOLNA

The Cave Chapel opposite the Gellért Baths was built in 1926 for the Pauline order. Its entrance was walled up during the Communist period, when the monasteries were persecuted and many of the monks killed or imprisoned.

✚ D10 ✉ XI, Gellért-hegy 🕐 Daily 8–8 (but closed to non-observants during Mass) 🚌 Bus: 27, 86; tram: 18, 19, 41, 118 ♿ None ✋ Free

St. Anna Church

Király Thermal Baths

Waterside Walk

This walk allows you to explore Margaret Island and the main sights of the Víziváros (Water Town) along the river bank.

DISTANCE: 6km (4 miles) **ALLOW:** 2–3 hours

START

MARGIT HÍD
C5 Bus: 6, 26, 91, 191; tram: 4, 6

END

GELLÉRT TÉR
D10 Bus: 27, 86; tram: 18, 19, 41, 118

❶ Join the walkway leading to Margit-sziget (▷ 42) from the bridge. Follow the main path past the Centenary Monument, the fountain (which periodically plays classical music) and ruins of the Franciscan church.

❷ Turn right at the next narrow path and take a swift turn around the Rose Garden to the left. Return to the path and continue to the eastern side of the island.

❸ Turn left if you want to see the ruins of the Dominican church and Premonstratensian Chapel; otherwise turn right and return to the bridge.

❹ Turn right and leave the bridge down steps to the right. Cross under the bridge and follow Bem József utca before turning left on to Fő utca.

❽ On arriving at Gellért tér, take a look inside the Cave Chapel (▷ 46) before ducking into the Gellért Baths (▷ 41) for a well-earned soak.

❼ Cross Clark Ádám tér and join Várkert rakpart. The next stretch of the walk offers good river views. As you reach Elizabeth Bridge, look up to the statue of Gellért (▷ 45). Pass beneath Elizabeth Bridge and continue to follow the river.

❻ Walk south along Fő utca, passing the Király Baths (▷ 45), Batthyány tér (and St. Anna Church, ▷ 46), until you arrive at Clark Ádám tér. Take a moment to admire the Chain Bridge.

❺ This is the main street of the area known as Water Town.

Entertainment and Nightlife

FECSKE

www.fecske.net

Fecske is a newly opened terrace club on the roof of the Komjádi Swimming Baths.

B4 II, Árpád fejedelem útja 8 ☎ 326 0714 ⏰ May–Sep daily 10am–4pm (closed rest of year) 🚌 Bus: 6, 60, 86; tram: 17

RUDAS ROMKERT

The paved terrace outside the Rudas Baths is a good spot for a coffee during the day and a dance at night.

C9 XI, Döbrentei tér 9 ⏰ May–Sep Tue–Sat

ROCK THE BOAT

The A38 (www.a38.hu) has developed into a popular venue since its introduction to the cultural scene a few years ago. It is unusual in being an ex-industrial ship that was brought from Ukraine, and is permanently moored on the Buda bank near Petőfi Bridge. As well as hosting live-music events (check the website for the upcoming programme), it has a restaurant and nightclub.

E11 ☎ 464 3940 🚌 Bus: 12; tram: 4, 6

---

noon–4am, Sun–Mon noon–2am (closed rest of year) 🚌 Bus: 5, 7, 8, 78, 86, 112; tram: 18, 19, 41, 118

ZÖLD PARDON

www.zp.hu

Summer club on the southern side of the Petőfi bridgehead. The music played is primarily rock.

E11 XI, Goldmann György tér 6 ⏰ May–Sep daily 9pm–6am (closed rest of year) 🚌 Bus: 3, 12, 86; tram: 4, 6

Restaurants

PRICES

Prices are approximate, based on a 3-course meal for one person.

€€€	over 5,000Ft
€€	3,000–5,000Ft
€	under 3,000Ft

BÚSULÓ JUHÁSZ (€€€)

www.busulojuhasz.hu

Atmospheric restaurant with a pleasant tiered terrace and views of the Buda Hills. Located below the citadel on Gellért-hegy, it specializes in stews featuring rabbit, goose and duck.

B10 XI, Kelenhegyi út 58 ☎ 209 1649 ⏰ Daily 12–12 🚌 Bus: 27

MALOMTÓ (€€–€€€)

www.malomto.hu

The 'Water Mill Lake' stands opposite the Lukács Baths. It is modern and minimalist and serves well-rated international cuisine.

B4 II, Frankel Leó út 48 ☎ 336 1830 ⏰ Daily 12–12 🚌 Bus: 6; tram: 17

MARGITKERT (€–€€)

www.margitkert.com

The Margitkert is known for the live evening music of Lajos Baross,

the leading violinist of the Budapest Gypsy Symphony Orchestra. The Hungarian cuisine is filling.

B5 II, Margit utca 15 ☎ 326 0860 ⏰ Daily 12–12 🚌 Tram: 4, 6

TRÓFEA GRILL (€€)

www.trofeagrill.eu

Fixed-price all-you-can-eat buffet featuring traditional Hungarian food as well as a variety of international dishes.

B5 II, Margit körút 2 ☎ 438 9090 ⏰ Mon–Fri 12–12, Sat 11.30–12 🚌 Bus: 6, 26, 86, 91; tram: 4, 6, 17

It is in the area known as Leopold Town that the city's main financial, legal and spiritual strands meet. Here you'll find not only the Parliament building, but also St. Stephen's Basilica, home to the country's most holy relic.

Lipótváros (Parliament)

utca

Kres Géza utca

VÁCI ÚT

P

West End
City Center

**Nyugati
pályaudvar**

i

Podmaniczky

Csengery utca

Vörösmarty utca

Skála
Metro

TERÉZ

Szobi utca

Fényes

utca

Podmaniczky utca

Szondi utca

Weiner Leó utca

József

KÖRÚT

utca

i

Lovag utca

P

Nagymező

6 utca

**Kolibri
Színház**

P

Dessewffy

Jenő utca

Mozsár utca

Zichy

Hajós utca

utca

**Fővárosi
Operettszínház**

6 utca

Lázár

utca

Dalszínház

**Magyar Állami
Operaház**

Opera

Révay

ANDRÁSSY

Paulay Ede utca

Postamúzeum

E   F

r Állami
náz

TOP 25

The grand State Opera House was contructed in the 19th century

LIPÓTVÁROS (PARLIAMENT) ★ **TOP 25**

THE BASICS

www.opera.hu

🔲 D7

✉ VI, Andrássy út 22

☎ 331 2550

🕐 Guided tours (in English) daily at 3 and 4. Groups by appointment

☎ 332 8197

Ⓜ Opera

🚌 Bus: 4; trolley-bus: 70, 78

♿ Good (but call in advance to arrange a tour)

💷 Guided tour: moderate

DID YOU KNOW?

● The auditorium holds nearly 1,300 spectators.

● During restoration in the 1990s, 300,000 pieces of gold leaf were used in replacing the gilding.

● The auditorium's chandelier weighs around three tonnes.

The Budapest State Opera House is one of the most sumptuous buildings in the capital. Tickets are excellent value, but even if you don't take in a performance it's well worth a peek inside.

Size isn't everything When Ferenc József agreed to fund the construction of the opera house he ordered that it be smaller than its equivalent in Vienna. Miklós Ybl followed his wishes to the letter, but he succeeded in upstaging the Austrian capital in another way: the (probably fanciful) story goes that when the emperor saw the finished building he regretted he hadn't mentioned that it should also be less beautiful. Ybl was painstakingly meticulous and the building process took nearly a decade. Ferenc Erkel, the 'father of Hungarian opera' and composer of the national anthem, conducted two of his creations (*Bánk Bán* and *Hunyadi László*) on the opening day in 1884. Among big names to have served as director are Gustav Mahler and Otto Klemperer.

The decoration On approaching the neo-Renaissance building you'll see statues of Ferenc Erkel and Ferenc Liszt either side of the entrance, as well as the figures of other great composers (including Beethoven and Mozart) above the balcony on the first floor. Inside is a grand staircase leading to the auditorium, which is painted in rich red and gilded with gold leaf. The frescoes are by leading Historicist artists Károly Lotz, Bertalan Székely and Mór Than.

Néprajzi Múzeum

The Museum of Ethnography was built to house the Supreme Court

The Museum of Ethnography often gets overlooked, but it's actually one of the city's most vibrant collections. The permanent exhibition is devoted to traditional dress and crafts, and there are frequently interesting temporary displays.

The history The story behind the birth of the building is an interesting one. In the 1880s, a competition was held to design the Parliament building, which was being erected to coincide with the millennial celebrations of 1896. Imre Steindl was the winner, but the runner-up designs weren't wasted: two of them were also constructed on Kossuth tér to house political and legal bodies—including this building by Alajos Hauszmann, which housed the Supreme Court for half a century.

The exhibition There's a certain mismatch between the high-blown nature of the building and the more earthy, vernacular items it contains. Many of these were gathered during a period of obsession with national identity (and, by extension, vernacular and folkloric arts and crafts) that emerged in the late 19th century. Thirteen rooms on the first floor hold objects relating to the life of the peasantry between the 18th century and World War I, including working tools, decorated furniture, everyday dress and festival costumes. There are also reconstructions of peasant houses from Transdanubia, as well as old film clips and sound recordings.

THE BASICS

www.neprajz.hu
➕ C6
✉ V, Kossuth Lajos tér 12
☎ 473 2400
🕐 Tue–Sun 10–6 (also open Whit Monday; closed 1 Jan, 24–26 Dec, 31 Dec)
🚇 Kossuth tér
🚌 Bus: 15; trolley-bus: 70, 78; tram: 2
♿ Good. Entrance via Szalay utca
💲 Permanent exhibition: free

HIGHLIGHTS

● Interior of early 19th-century peasant house from the Őrség region
● Decorated 19th-century kitchen from a rich farm house in the Sárköz region

Országház

DID YOU KNOW?

● The Parliament building is one of the largest in the world and took 17 years to complete.

● The building contains 250 statues, 40kg (88 lb) of gold and 40 million bricks.

TIPS

● Access is restricted when parliament is in session.

● If you are an EU citizen, you must produce your passport as proof at the ticket office.

You're unlikely to miss the looming Parliament building, which dominates the Pest bank at Kossuth tér and is a perennial feature of tourist brochures. Inside is the national symbol of Hungary —the Holy Crown.

The background Imre Steindl's neo-Gothic creation was the winning entry in the competition to build Parliament, the main project of several commissioned to coincide with the 1,000th anniversary of the Magyar arrival. Steindl was slightly lucky to have the opportunity—a previous competition in the 1840s had been won by Frigyes Feszl, but the 1848–49 Independence War meant the project never got off the ground. The influence of the Houses of Parliament in London is obvious in the thin,

pinnacled spires, but Steindl also introduced a round baroque central hall and a dome.

The interior On entering the building, you pass into a hall with eight enormous marble pillars. A sweeping staircase leads up to the main hall beneath the dome—look up to frescoes by Károly Lotz. In the middle of the hall stands a case containing the Holy Crown, sceptre, orb and sword. The crown, with its bent cross, is the primary feature of the country's coat of arms, and can be seen on the national flag. Tradition states that this was the crown given to King István in AD1000 by the pope, but it actually dates to the 12th century. The building features two near-identical chambers; only that to the south (the Chamber of Representatives) is now used for parliamentary business.

THE BASICS

www.mkogy.hu

+ C6

✉ V, Kossuth Lajos tér 1–3

☎ 441 4904

🕐 Guided tours only. In English daily at 10, 12, 2. Ticket office at Gate X

Ⓜ Kossuth tér

🚌 Bus: 15; trolley-bus: 70, 78; tram: 2

♿ Good (but telephone at least two days in advance to arrange assistance)

 Free for EU citizens, expensive for non-EU citizens

Szent István Bazilika

HIGHLIGHTS

● Views from the Panorama Tower
● Right hand of St. Stephen

TIP

● In the past, some tourists have been approached by fraudsters pretending to be church officials and asking for payment for admission to the church. The church is free of charge—it is only extra to enter the treasury or Panorama Tower.

St. Stephen's Basilica is the capital's largest church—although only the third-biggest in the country as a whole—and home to the Holy Right, the country's most sacred relic.

A troubled history The Basilica had difficult beginnings. It was originally designed by József Hild, who died in 1867 not only before his neoclassical creation was completed but before it collapsed (apparently because of low-grade building materials). Miklós Ybl took over the project, and conceived a neo-Renaissance church with a dome measuring 96m (315ft) in height—a conscious nod to the time of the Magyar arrival in AD896. He too died before the building was finished in 1906. There was extensive fire damage during World

The grand façade of St. Stephen's Basilica; an altar painting of Stephen offering his crown to the Virgin by Gyula Benczúr; the magnificent dome; detail of wooden and brass doors; entrance archway to the basilica (clockwise from left)

War II and restorations weren't finalized until 50 years later.

Inside the church The church interior takes the shape of a Greek cross, its floor laid with slabs of black and white marble. There is a fine statue of St. Stephen by Alajos Stróbl on the high altar, while the dome is decorated with mosaics by Károly Lotz. The object of most interest, however, is the mummified right hand of St. Stephen himself, the founder of the Christian state. The hand is held in a precious casket, and is illuminated on payment of a coin. The Panorama Tower—an exterior gallery running around the base of the dome—offers lovely city views. You can climb steps the whole distance to the gallery or take a lift two-thirds of the way.

THE BASICS

www.basilica.hu
+ D7
✉ V, Szent István tér
☎ 403 5370
🕐 Mon–Fri 9–5, Sat 9–1, Sun 1–5
Ⓜ Bajcsy Zsilinszky utca, Deák tér, Arany János utca
🚌 Bus: 15; trolley-bus: 70, 72, 73, 78
♿ Good
💶 Church: free; treasury, Panorama Tower: inexpensive
❓ Guided tours available

More to See

GRESHAM PALOTA
www.fourseasons.com/budapest
The Gresham Palace now houses the Four Seasons Hotel (▷ 112)—Hungary's most exclusive—but it was originally built as the offices of an English insurance company in the early 20th century.
⊞ C8 ✉ V, Roosevelt tér 5–6 ☎ 268 6000 🍴 Restaurant and café facilities 🚇 Kossuth tér, Vörösmarty tér 🚌 Bus: 4, 15, 16, 105; tram: 2, 2A ♿ Very good

KOSSUTH LAJOS TÉR
Kossuth tér holds the Parliament building and is named after the leader of the 1848 uprising against Habsburg rule. An eternal flame commemorates the victims of the notorious 1956 Uprising, which was suppressed by Soviet tanks.
⊞ C6 🚇 Kossuth tér 🚌 Bus: 15; trolley-bus: 70, 78; tram: 2, 2A ♿ Good

MAGYAR TUDOMÁNYOS AKADÉMIA
www.mta.hu
The Hungarian Academy of Sciences is housed in a neo-Renaissance palace, and was founded by the great reformer István Széchenyi in the early 19th century.
⊞ C7 ✉ V, Roosevelt tér 9 ☎ 411 6100 🚇 Kossuth tér, Vörösmarty tér 🚌 Bus: 4, 15, 16, 105; tram: 2, 2A

NYUGATI PÁLYAUDVAR
The Western Railway Station was the city's first. It was completed in 1877 and was designed by the company run by Gustave Eiffel (of Eiffel Tower fame).
⊞ D6 ✉ VI, Teréz körút 55–57 🍴 Restaurant and café facilities 🚇 Nyugati pályaudvar 🚌 Bus: 6, 26, 91, 191; trolley-bus: 72, 73; tram: 4, 6

SZABADSÁG TÉR
In the past Freedom Square was the site of an army barracks. Lajos Batthyány, prime minister of the independent government during the 1848–49 Independence War, was executed here.
⊞ C7 🚇 Kossuth tér 🚌 Bus: 15; trolley-bus: 70, 78; tram: 2, 2A

The façade of Gresham Palace

Soviet Memorial on Szabadság tér

Shopping

AJKA KRISTÁLY

This is an outlet selling the famous Ajka crystal products.

🔲 D6 ✉ XIII, Szent István körút 18 ☎ 340 5083 🕐 Mon–Fri 10–6, Sat 10–1 🚇 Nyugati pályaudvar 🚃 Tram: 2, 4, 6

ANDRÁSSY ÚT

The first section of the city's main avenue is dotted with a few shops along its way, including clothes boutiques, stores selling crystal, porcelain and jewellery, and several bookshops (including the Bibliotéka Antikvárium at the end nearest the heart of the city, which stocks antiquarian books).

🔲 D8–E6 ✉ VI, Andrássy út 🕐 Shops generally open Mon–Fri 10–6, Sat 10–2 🚇 Oktogon, Opera, Bajcsy-Zsilinszky út

ELSŐ MAGYAR BORHÁZ RT

www.borbazilika.com
This quality-wine shop in a 19th-century house near the Basilica (▷ 56–57) offers vintage Hungarian wines dating back to 1964 and also has a wine museum in its large cellar system.

🔲 D7 ✉ V, Bajcsy-Zsilinszky út 18 ☎ 301 0699 🕐 Mon–Fri 10–6, Sat 10–1 🚇 Bajcsy-Zsilinszky út 🚃 4; trolley-bus: 72, 73

FALK MIKSA UTCA

Running north from Kossuth tér as far as Szent István körút, this streets holds the best of Budapest's antiques shops. There are dozens of stores along its length, selling furniture, art, jewellery and porcelain.

🔲 C6 🕐 Shops generally Mon–Fri 10–6, Sat 10–2 🚇 Kossuth tér; tram: 2, 4, 6

LEHEL MARKET

You won't miss this market in its bright building designed to look like a ship. It sells fresh food and wines.

🔲 D5 ✉ XIII, Váci út 7–15 ☎ 288 6887 🕐 Mon–Fri 6–6, Sat 6–2, Sun 6–1 🚇 Lehel tér 🚃 Trolley-bus: 76; tram: 14

BULL'S BLOOD

One of Hungary's most famous wines is called Bull's Blood (Bikavér), produced in Szekszárd and Eger. Its name dates to the famous siege of Eger Castle in 1552. A small number of Hungarian soldiers succeeded in repelling a Turkish force 40 times larger. They drank red wine to steel their nerves, but from a distance the Turks became convinced it was bull's blood—and that this was the secret behind their superhuman strength.

SZENT ISTVÁN TÉR

The square in front of St. Stephen's Basilica (▷ 56–57) has a couple of gift shops. Items for sale include embroidered tablecloths and other handcrafted goods.

🔲 D7 🕐 Shops generally Mon–Fri 10–6, Sat 10–2 🚇 Arany János utca 🚃 Trolley-bus: 72, 73

WESTEND SHOPPING CENTER

www.westend.hu
Located close to the Western Railway Station (▷ 58) on the broad and straight Váci út, the Westend is a massive shopping mall packed with hundreds of stores (selling books, clothes, jewellery, sports goods and much more), bars and restaurants, a cinema and even a large roof garden (where there is an ice rink in winter).

🔲 D5–6 ✉ VI, Váci út 1–3 ☎ 374 6573 🕐 Shops open Mon–Sat 10–8, Sun 10–6 🚇 Nyugati pályaudvar 🚌 Bus: 6, 26, 91, 191; trolley-bus: 72, 73; tram: 4, 6, 14

LIPÓTVÁROS (PARLIAMENT)

SHOPPING

59

Entertainment and Nightlife

BANK DANCE HALL

www.bankdancehall.hu
This well-established nightclub in the same building as the Western Railway Station is preferred by the younger crowd. Dancers writhe in a large main hall.
🔀 D6 ✉ VI, Teréz körút 55 ☎ 20 3444 888 ⏰ Sun–Thu 10pm–4am, Fri–Sat 10pm–5am 🚇 Nyugati pályaudvar 🚌 Bus: 6, 26, 91, 191; trolley-bus: 72, 73; tram: 4, 6, 14

BECKETTS

www.becketts.hu
This Irish pub—named after Samuel Beckett—is very popular with expats and is particularly crowded during international sports matches (when it has several screens showing the football or rugby).
🔀 D6 ✉ V, Bajcsy-Zsilinszky út 72 ☎ 311 1035 ⏰ Mon–Thu noon–1am, Fri–Sun noon–2am 🚇 Nyugati pályaudvar 🚌 Trolley-bus: 70, 72, 73, 78

BOX UTCA

www.box-utca.hu
Established in 2002 by a Hungarian World Champion boxer, Box utca is an elegant bar and restaurant with plenty of TV screens for sports events.
🔀 D7 ✉ VI, Bajcsy-Zsilinszky út 21 ☎ 354 1444 ⏰ Mon–Fri 8am–12am, Sat–Sun 10am–12am 🚇 Arany János utca 🚌 Trolley-bus: 72, 73

LAS VEGAS CASINO

www.lasvegascasino.hu
You can gamble the night away in this casino in the Sofitel Budapest Hotel, near the Chain Bridge.
🔀 C8 ✉ V, Roosevelt tér 2 ☎ 317 6022 ⏰ Daily 2pm–5am 🚌 Bus: 4, 15, 16, 105; tram: 2, 2A

MAGYAR ÁLLAMI OPERHÁZ

www.opera.hu
The Hungarian State Opera House looks beautiful in itself (▷ 52), but if you have the chance it's definitely worth listening to a performance and enjoying the superb acoustics. The tickets are extremely cheap by Western standards.
🔀 D7 ✉ VI, Andrássy út 22 ☎ 332 7914

ISTVÁN 'KO KO' KOVÁCS

As an amateur boxer, István 'Ko-Ko' Kovács—the owner of Box utca—took a bronze at the 1992 Olympics and then gold (as a bantamweight) four years later. After turning professional in 1997, he enjoyed an unbeaten run of 20 bouts, culminating in his capture of the WBO featherweight title (vacated by Naseem Hamed) by defeating Antonio Diaz. He lost the title in his next fight, and retired shortly afterwards in 2002.

⏰ Performances Tue–Sun (closed Mon); ticket office open until 5 (or start of performance) 🚇 Opera 🚌 Bus: 4

MORRISON'S MUSIC PUB

www.morrisons.hu
This popular pub near the Opera House (▷ 52) has a dance floor and karaoke nights on Wednesdays. A sister bar—Morrison's Music Pub 2—recently opened at Honvéd utca 40, and has nightly live music.
🔀 D7 ✉ VI, Révay utca 25 ☎ 269 4060 ⏰ Daily 5–4 🚇 Opera 🚌 Bus: 4

MOULIN ROUGE

www.moulinrouge.hu
In the same building as the Operettszínház (▷ 61), the Moulin Rouge offers dining in the restaurant and then an extravagant revue show (after which the punters themselves can dance to live music) on Friday and Saturday, and a nightclub on Wednesday.
🔀 D7 ✉ VI, Nagymező utca 17 ☎ 30 434 9995 ⏰ Wed 10pm–4am, Fri–Sat 8pm–4am 🚇 Opera 🚌 Trolley-bus: 70, 78

MŰVÉSZ CINEMA

www.artmozi.hu
The 'Artist' cinema shows popular and cult films. Small stalls in the entrance lobby also sell CDs, books and jewellery.

🚇 D6 ✉ VI, Teréz körút 30
☎ 332 6726 🎫 Screenings
daily 🚇 Oktogon
🚎 Trolley-bus: 4, 6

NEGRO

Apparently named after
a cough sweet, Negro
stands in the shadow
of St. Stephen's Basilica
(▷ 56–57) and is
Budapest's most chic
wine and cocktail bar.
The outdoor seating on
the square is lovely in
summer. It also serves
decent food.
🚇 D7 ✉ V, Szent István tér

11 ☎ 373 0391
🎫 Mon–Tue 8pm–1am,
Wed–Sun 8pm–2am 🚇 Deák
tér 🚎 Trolley-bus: 72, 73

NEW ORLEANS JAZZ CLUB

www.neworleans.hu
This smooth club hosts
good live jazz acts
every evening except
Sunday and Monday.
Performances start at
around 9.
🚇 D7 ✉ VI, Lovag utca 5
☎ 451 7525 🎫 Daily
6pm–2am 🚎 Trolley-bus:
70, 78

OPERETTSZÍNHÁZ

www.operettszinhaz.hu
This is the leading spot
to take in a light
musical, for which
Hungary is well known.
The art nouveau décor
is impressive and there
are English subtitles
for some of the
performances.
🚇 D7 ✉ VI, Nagymező utca
17 ☎ 269 3870
🎫 Performances daily
🚇 Opera 🚎 Trolley-bus:
70, 78

Restaurants

BIARRITZ (€€€)

www.biarritz.hu
This restaurant has a
long tradition—dating
back to the interwar
years—and an equally
long-standing reputation
for international cuisine.
🚇 C7 ✉ V, Kossuth tér 18
☎ 311 4413 🎫 Mon–Fri
9am–11pm, Sat–Sun
10am–11pm 🚇 Kossuth tér
🚎 Trolley-bus: 70, 78; tram:
2, 2A

CAFÉ KÖR (€€)

www.cafekor.hu
One of the city's lead-
ing restaurants, Café
Kör serves lighter takes
on Hungarian classic

dishes, as well as inter-
national choices. Given
the quality, the food is
well priced.
🚇 D7 ✉ V, Sas utca 17
☎ 311 0053 🎫 Mon–Sat
10–10 🚇 Arany János utca
🚎 Bus: 15; trolley-bus:
72, 73

CALLAS (€€€)

This elegant restaurant
stands next to the
Opera House, and is
therefore popular with
those attending
performances here and
at other venues in the
nearby theatre district.
🚇 D7 ✉ VI, Andrássy út
20 ☎ 354 0954 🎫 Daily
12–3, 6–11 🚇 Opera
🚎 Bus: 4

EURÓPA KÁVÉHÁZ (€€)

www.europakavehaz.hu
Graceful coffeehouse beside the Vígszínház with a wide selection of traditional pastries and desserts, as well as lighter cakes. It also offers a selection of sandwiches and salads, and there's an adjacent, less expensive pâtisserie specializing in cakes.

🔹 D5 ✉ V, Szent István körút 7–9 ☎ 312 2362
🕐 May–Oct 9am–11pm, Nov–Apr 9am–10pm 🚌 Bus: 26, 91, 191; tram: 4, 6

KÉT SZERECSEN (€€)

www.ketszerecsen.hu
This atmospheric restaurant—the 'Two Saracens'—near the various theatres on Nagymező utca offers some good people-watching tables and tasty Mediterranean dishes such as risotto. The restaurant is also open daily for breakfast.

🔹 D7 ✉ VI, Nagymező utca 14 ☎ 343 1984
🕐 Mon–Fri 8am–1am, Sat–Sun 9am–1am
🚇 Opera 🚌 Bus: 4; trolley-bus: 70, 78

MOKKA (€€€)

www.mokkarestaurant.hu
The top-quality Mokka is located near the Basilica (▷ 56–57). Its menu draws on a range of international influences, the décor has terra-cotta hues and a Moroccan feel, and the service is impressive.

🔹 D7 ✉ V, Sas utca 4 ☎ 328 0081 🕐 Daily 12–12
🚇 Deák tér

NÁDOR (€€)

Nádor is a bright restaurant near Parliament (▷ 54–55). It serves a choice of Hungarian and international food, and the dishes are satisfying both in size and price.

🔹 C7 ✉ V, Nádor utca 30 ☎ 302 3086 🕐 Daily 12–11
🚇 Kossuth tér 🚌 Bus: 15; trolley-bus: 70, 78; tram: 2, 2A

PÁVA (€€€)

www.fourseasons.com/budapest
'The Peacock' is the restaurant of the luxurious Four Seasons Hotel and specializes in contemporary Italian cuisine. Its position affords pleasant views across Roosevelt tér to the river.

🔹 C8 ✉ V, Roosevelt tér 5–6 ☎ 268 8000
🕐 Mon–Sat 6pm–10.30pm
🚌 Bus: 4, 15, 16, 105; tram: 2, 2A

SEGAL (€€€)

Owned and run by French chef Victor Segal, this chic sister restaurant of the well-regarded Baraka serves innovative cuisine fusing French and Asian influences. Among the more surprising creations are chocolate mousse with salt and black pepper and beef with fried, salted pear.

🔹 D6 ✉ VI, Ó utca 43–49 ☎ 354 7888 🕐 Daily 7am–2am 🚇 Oktogon; bus: 4; trolley-bus: 70; tram: 4, 6

TRATTORIA POMO D'ORO (€€)

www.pomodorobudapest.com
This Italian trattoria prides itself on fresh ingredients, traditional and original dishes. It has a list of over 100 wines.

🔹 C7 ✉ V, Arany János utca 9 ☎ 302 6473
🕐 Mon–Fri 11am–midnight, Sat–Sun 12–12 🚇 Arany János utca 🚌 Bus: 15; trolley-bus: 72, 73

GOULASH

The dish for which Hungary is famous around the world is, of course, goulash—or, more properly, *gulyás* (pronounced goo-yash). Strictly a soup rather than a stew (a stew is called *pörkölt*), it was the traditional fare of herders (*gulyás* means 'cattle herder') on the plains who cooked the dish in large kettle cauldrons. It is usually made of beef, peppers, paprika, onions and potatoes, and is mildly spicy (although far from as fiery as many expect).

The Belváros—or inner city—is Pest's focal point. It falls within District V and is largely contained by the river on its western side and the Small Boulevard (Kiskörút), which arcs from Széchenyi lánchíd to Szabadság híd.

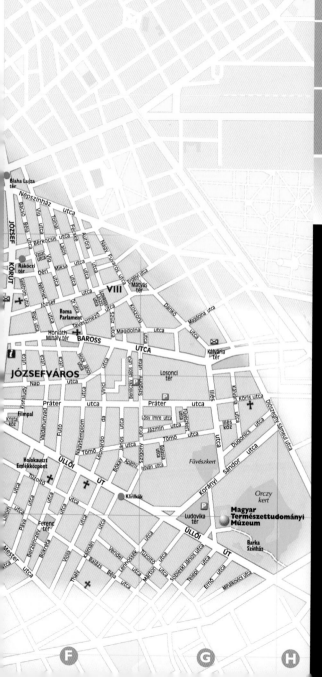

Blaha Lujza tér

Népszínház utca

Rákóczi tér

JÓZSEF
KÖRÚT

VIII

Roma Parlament

Horváth Mihály tér

BAROSS UTCA

JÓZSEFVÁROS

Nap utca

Filmpal

Kristal köz

Práter utca

Práter utca

Losonci tér

Holokauszt Emlékközpont

ÜLLŐI ÚT

Klinikák

Füvészkert

Korányi Sándor

Orczy kert

Ludovika tér

Magyar Természettudományi Múzeum

Barka Színház

ÜLLŐI ÚT

F   G   H

Danube Boat Trip

TOP
25

There are up to eight cruises a day and three an evening during high season

THE BASICS

www.legenda.hu

⊞ C8

✉ Boats depart from Vigadó tér, pier 7

☎ 266 4190

🕐 *Duna Bella* during the day, *Duna Legenda* in the evening (no tours 24–26 Dec). For timetable details, visit the website

Ⓜ Vörösmarty tér

🚌 Bus: 15; tram: 2

♿ Good

💷 Moderate

HIGHLIGHT

● The illuminations during an evening cruise—particularly the bridges, Parliament and palace

TIP

● The evening option lasts an hour, while you can choose between one- and two-hour tours during the day (the latter including a stop-off for a walk on Margaret Island).

The Danube is the city's life blood, and many of the best sights are ranged along each of its banks. A boat trip is a good way to get the most from the riverscape—itself a UNESCO World Heritage Site.

The options The company Legenda offers two standard tours (daytime and evening) aboard its boats the *Duna Bella* and *Duna Legenda*. Passengers listen to an audioguide commentary (available in a choice of 30 languages). The boats depart from a pier at Vigadó tér, heading north up to (and, during the day, around) Margaret Island before moving southward again as far as Petőfi Bridge and back to their starting point.

What you'll see On leaving Vigadó tér, you'll move beneath the Chain Bridge and on past the Academy of Sciences and Parliament on your right before reaching Margaret Island. On the way back down, look out for the spire of the Calvinist church on the western bank and behind that, on Castle Hill, Mátyás Church and the turrets of the Fishermen's Bastion. Once back under the Chain Bridge, look up to Buda Castle Palace and then the Gellért Statue looming over Elizabeth Bridge. At the other side of the bridge is the Inner City Parish Church. The Rudas Baths appear next on your right, while at the top of Gellért Hill is the Freedom Monument and Citadel. After passing the Géllert Hotel the boat will return home.

The ceiling in the entrance hall (left); beautiful Zsolnay tiling (right)

Iparművé...
Mú...

The building containing the Museum of Applied Arts is arguably more of a draw than its collections. It represents one of the country's leading examples of Secessionist architecture, and is a celebration of this turn-of-the-century style.

The building Budapest's Museum of Applied Arts was only the third of its kind in Europe, its collection originally based upon purchases of industrial items for display at Vienna's World Exhibition of 1873. In 1890 a competition was opened for architects to design a dedicated building for the museum as part of the 1896 millennial celebrations. The winners were Ödön Lechner and Gyula Pártos, and the final result is regarded as a masterpiece of Lechner's lifelong dedication to creating a style uniquely Hungarian. On completion, there was widespread outrage at its extravagance and, particularly, its use of eastern themes (which drew upon contemporary theories about Hungarians having Indian ancestry) that were criticized as being a celebration of 'gypsies'. The design blends folksy, Islamic and Hindu motifs, and makes extensive use of glazed Zsolnay ceramics.

The exhibits There are no permanent exhibitions at the museum. Instead several temporary displays are put on show over the three floors at any one time, some pulled from the museum's own holdings and others borrowed from elsewhere.

THE BASICS

www.imm.hu
+ E10
✉ IX, Üllői út 33–37
☎ 456 5100
🕐 Tue–Sun 10–6
Ⓜ Ferenc körút
🚋 Tram: 4, 6
♿ Good
💷 Prices vary according to exhibition

HIGHLIGHTS

● The Zsolnay majolica features decorating the walls of the museum's portico
● The striking domed roof, its Zsolnay tiles—in a diamond pattern of green and gold—visible from afar

AROUND BELVÁROS ★ **TOP 25**

TOP 25

Magyar Nemzeti Múzeum

HIGHLIGHTS

● The Hungarian corona-
tion mantle
● Mosaic floor excavated
from a Roman villa in
western Hungary (the
Roman lapidarium)
● 18th-century woven
wall hanging depicting the
liberation of Buda (room 8)

TIP

● Be sure to take a look
at the fabulous allegorical
and historical paintings
(by 19th-century painters
Mór Than and Károly Lotz)
on the walls and ceiling of
the main staircase.

**The Hungarian National Museum is the
largest in the country. The exhibits are
fascinating, among them the coronation
cloak of King Stephen I.**

History Housed in a neoclassical pile designed by Mihály Pollack and completed in 1847,
the museum was brought into being by the
great reformer Ferenc Széchényi. In the early
years of the 19th century, the count donated
his vast collection of prints, manuscripts,
books and maps to the country, and these
formed the core of the museum's holdings.
The grounds form the backdrop to the annual
Independence Day celebrations on 15 March.
It was from the museum steps here on that
day in 1848 that poet Sándor Petőfi addressed
a crowd with his *National Song* exhorting

A skeleton of an elephant (left) is just one of the exhibits in the Hungarian National Museum (below left and right)

THE BASICS

www.mnm.hu
+ E9
✉ VIII, Múzeum körút 14–16
☎ 327 7773
🕐 Tue–Sun 10–6
🍴 Café facilities
Ⓜ Kálvin tér, Astoria
🚌 Bus: 7, 9, 15, 73, 78; tram: 47, 49
♿ Access via side entrance on Bródy Sándor utca, where there is a lift. Phone in advance for further assistance
💰 Free (permanent exhibitions) or moderate (temporary exhibitions)
❓ Audio tours available, as well as guided tours by advance appointment

Hungarians to throw off the grip of their Habsburg rulers. This was one of the sparks for the Independence War of 1848–49, in which the Habsburgs eventually proved victorious. Petőfi himself was killed during battle the following year.

The exhibitions Among the permanent exhibitions are a Roman lapidarium and display of medieval stone sculptures in the basement level. On the ground floor—to the left of the entrance hall—is the museum's prize exhibit. The coronation cloak belonging to King Stephen I is a sumptuous piece of embroidered silk. The upper floors trawl through a thousand years of history, starting with the period of Árpád rule and concluding with the departure of the last Soviets in 1990.

Nagy Zsinagóga and Zsido Múzeum

DID YOU KNOW?

● Only New York's synagogue is bigger than that in Budapest.
● It suffered damage during the war. Renovation in the 1990s was in part funded by a foundation led by the actor Tony Curtis, whose father was a Hungarian Jew.

TIP

● If you can, pay a visit to the synagogue during the Jewish Summer Festival when there are concerts held inside as part of a wider celebration of culture, music and dance.

The Great Synagogue is the second-largest synagogue in the world. It is a beautiful and imaginative piece of architecture, while its adjacent museum represents a moving reminder of the Holocaust in Hungary.

The Great Synagogue It's impossible to miss the massive, twin-towered Great Synagogue standing on the northern side of Dohány utca. It was built for both Orthodox and Reform Jews, and was finished in 1859. The designer was the Austrian architect Ludwig Förster, and he created an eclectic building topped with Moorish onion domes. The interior is heavily gilded and has separate seating for male and female worshippers. Behind the synagogue is a memorial park on

*Nagy Zsinagóga (Great Synagogue); Jewish tombstones; the façade o
synagogue; detail of one of the domes (clockwise from left)*

the burial place of many Jews who died of disease and starvation during the period when this area of the city was sealed off as a ghetto. A silver weeping willow sculpted by Imre Varga commemorates the victims.

Jewish Museum The Holocaust hit Hungary in March 1944, when the Germans occupied the country and put the Arrow-Cross Party (the Hungarian Nazis) in control. Over 600,000 of Hungary's Jews were killed or moved to concentration camps. The full programme of deportation from Budapest began in late 1944. Half the city's Jews died before the capital was liberated. The Jewish Museum contains an exhibition devoted to this period with contemporary photographs. There is also a collection of items relating to Jewish festivals.

THE BASICS

www.bpjewmus.hu
* D8 and E8
* VII, Dohány utca 2
* 342 8949
* Synagogue:
Mon–Thu 10–5, Fri 10–3,
Sun 10–2; museum:
Sun–Thu 10–6, Fri 10–3
* Astoria, Deák tér
* Bus: 7, 7A, 78; trolley-bus: 74; tram: 47, 49
* Synagogue: good;
museum: none
* Moderate
* Tours available

Váci utca

THE BASICS

* D9
* Shops generally daily 10–6
* Several cafés, bars and restaurants
* Vörösmarty tér, Ferenciek tere
* Bus: 5, 7, red 7, 15, 78, 112, red 173; tram: 2, 2A, 47, 49
* Vigadó tér
* Very good

HIGHLIGHTS

* Thonet House (No. 11)
* City Council Chamber (Nos. 62–64), designed by Imre Steindl in 1870
* Fountain with the statue of the 'Fisher Girl' in Kristóf tér
* White cobbles crossing the street and marking the position of the medieval northern gate to the city (demolished at the end of the 18th century)

Váci utca is the city's best-known street, and is the most central of the tourist arteries. Lined with cafés, bars and shops selling clothes, jewellery, glass and books, it usually thrums with people browsing or taking a stroll.

The street Running parallel to the river (although out of sight of it), Váci utca lasts much of the way through the Belváros. In medieval times, this was the full length of the city of Pest. It has been a spot to promenade and shop since the 18th century, and reached the height of its popularity among the fashionable set in the late 1800s and early 1900s. It was at this time that some of the elegant buildings were constructed, including the Thonet House (at No. 11)—designed by Ödön Lechner, the leading member of the Hungarian art nouveau movement. Some of the original character was sacrificed during communist 'modernization', but the pedestrianized street has enjoyed something of a renaissance in recent years with the appearance of boutiques representing Western designer chains.

Top to tail Two of the city's highlights can be found at either end of Váci utca. Facing the southern end, across Vámház körút, is the Great Market Hall (▷ 75). The northern end opens into Vörösmarty tér. A Christmas market (▷ 77) occupies the square in winter, and it is the permanent home of Gerbeaud (▷ panel, 82), the city's most famous coffeehouse.

BELVÁROSI PLÉBÁNIA TEMPLOM

The Inner City Parish Church is wedged into a tight space beside the Elizabeth Bridge. There was once a Roman fort here—a defensive post across the river from the main town of Aquincum (▷ 102). A church was built in the 11th century (and Bishop Gellért laid to rest inside after being murdered by pagans in the aftermath of King Stephen I's death), but the foundations of the present church date to the 12th century. The sanctuary is medieval; there is a Turkish prayer niche inside, evidence that the Ottomans used it as a place of worship during their occupation.

🚇 D9 ✉ V, Március 15 tér ☎ 318 3108 🕐 Mon–Fri 9–7 🚇 Ferenciek tere 🚌 Bus: 5, 7, 8, 15, 78, 112, 173; tram: 2, 2A 🚹 Good 🎫 Free

DUNAKORZÓ

The Pest-side Danube promenade is a popular strolling street running from Elizabeth Bridge up to the Chain Bridge, with the tram tracks running just below it. Along the way you'll pass the extravagant 19th-century Vigadó theatre, which hosted musical greats like Liszt and Wagner. Look out too for the statue of the 'Little Princess' sitting on the railings; it was placed here in 1989 and is a popular subject of tourist photographs, with the palace facing it across the river.

🚇 C8 🍴 Restaurant and café facilities 🚇 Vörösmarty tér 🚌 Bus: 15; tram: 2, 2A 🚹 Good

FERENCES TEMPLOM

http://pestiferences.ofm.hu

The original 13th-century church on this site was destroyed by the Turks in 1526, after which the Franciscans rebuilt it—only for the Turks to appropriate it as a mosque when they returned and occupied the country for the next 150 years. The current version is 18th-century, with ceiling paintings added later by Károly Lotz. One of the pews here was where Franz Liszt used

The Danube Promenade between the Elizabeth and Chain bridges

Inner City Parish Church

to sit when he stayed in the presbytery in the late 1860s and early 1870s.

On the outside of the church is a stone-carved relief of a man pulling citizens into a small rowing boat. This is Miklós Wesselényi, an aristocrat who took to the water during the huge flood that devastated Pest in 1838, and saved a good number of lives by ferrying people away from danger.

🕂 D9 ⊠ V, Ferenciek tere 9
☎ 317 3322 🕓 Daily 6–12, 4–7
🚇 Ferenciek tere 🚌 Bus: 5, 7, 8, 15, 78, 112, 173; tram: 2, 2A 🚻 Good 🎟 Free

FÖLDALATTI VASÚTI MÚZEUM

The diminutive railway museum is housed in a preserved old station platform (complete with all its original fittings) in the Deák tér underpass. This was only the second underground railway line built in the world (after London). Note the old train carriages and the quaint wall tiles made by the

Zsolnay factory in Pécs (▷ panel, 78).

🕂 D8 ⊠ Deák tér, underpass ☎ 461 6500 🕓 Tue–Sun 10–5 🚇 Deák tér
🚌 Bus: 4, 9, 15, 105; tram 47, 49
🚻 None 🎟 Inexpensive

MAGYAR TERMÉSZETTUDOMÁNYI MÚZEUM

www.nhmus.hu

The Natural History Museum stands a few kilometres to the southeast of the Belváros along Üllői út. There's an outdoor geological park adjacent to the museum building (displaying rocks in chronological order, the oldest of which dates back a couple of hundred million years), while inside is a two-tonne skeleton of a whale (bearing scorch marks from a fire in 1956), an African diorama (featuring a real lake, and stuffed examples of animals including the Nile crocodile and king python), a superb coral-reef display (spread over 120 square metres beneath a

The spire of Ferences templom (left); statue on the church (right)

glass floor, and with 200 types of coral, 160 fish and over 1,000 kinds of snail, crab and other marine life) and an exhibition charting the human use of resources from the very early period of history and the impact this has had upon the natural world.

➕ G11 ✉ VIII, Ludovika tér 2–6 ☎ 210 1085 ⏰ Wed–Mon 10–6 (closed 24–26 Dec, 31 Dec, 1–2 Jan) 🍴 Café facilities 🚇 Klinikák; Nagyvárad tér 🚊 Tram: 24 ♿ Good ✋ Free

NAGYCSARNOK

Constructed at the end of the 19th century, the Great Market Hall is a Pest institution, an art nouveau behemoth facing the southern opening of Váci utca. It is impressive from the outside, with its patterned roof, while inside there are stalls spread over three floors (▷ 78). On the ground and basement levels you'll find a wide range of food and drink, including fresh vegetables, fish and meat, jars of pickles and caviar, tins of goose liver and bottles of wine and fruit brandy. The top floor is dedicated to craft works and embroidered lace, and also has some snack shacks and a buffet restaurant.

➕ D10 ✉ IX, Fővám tér 1–3 ⏰ Mon 6–5, Tue–Fri 6–6, Sat 6–2 🍴 Restaurant facilities 🚇 Kálvin tér 🚌 Bus: 15; trolley-bus: 83; tram: 47, 49 ♿ Good ✋ Free

REFORMÁTUS TEMPLOM

The design of the Calvinist Church in the busy traffic junction that is Kálvin tér was begun by József Hofrichter in 1816 and continued by József Hild. Its white, neoclassical exterior has an imposing portico, while inside the domed ceiling is barrel vaulted.

➕ E9 ✉ IX, Kálvin tér 7 ☎ 217 6769 ⏰ Daily 8–12, 4–6 🚇 Kálvin tér 🚌 Bus: 9, 15; tram: 47, 49 ♿ Good ✋ Free

Great Market Hall

Pest Promenade

This walk covers some choice portions of the heart of the city, including the main square and the river promenade.

DISTANCE: 4km (2.5 miles) **ALLOW:** 1.5–2 hours

START

VÖRÖSMARTY TÉR
🚇 C8 🚇 Vörösmarty tér

END

ROOSEVELT TÉR 🚇 C8
🚌 Bus: red 4, 15, 16, 105; tram: 2, 2A

❶ Begin your walk in Vörösmarty tér, the main square of the Belváros. Prepare with a coffee and cake in the famous Gerbeaud café (▷ panel, 82).

❽ Finish your walk in Roosevelt tér, dominated by the Chain Bridge and the Gresham Palace (▷ 58).

❷ Move south from the square along Váci utca (▷ 72), with its classy boutiques and bookshops. Look out for the statue of the 'Fisher Girl' in Kristóf tér and the white cobbles marking the medieval northern city gate.

❼ Once you reach the Freedom Bridge, join the riverside promenade and head north again. Enjoy the view of the Buda palace, and look out for the Inner City Parish Church (▷ 73) beside Elizabeth Bridge, the Vigadó theatre farther up and the statue of the 'Little Princess' on the railings.

❸ At the end of Váci utca's northern stretch, turn left on to Szabadsajtó útja. Walk past the Párisi udvar, popping your head in to admire the highly ornamental decor.

❻ Cross Kálvin tér, stopping to look at the Calvinist church. Join Vámház körút and follow it back toward the river. Shortly before you reach Freedom Bridge, you'll pass the Great Market Hall (▷ 75) on your left.

❹ Move on to Ferenciek tere with its Franciscan church across the road (▷ 73). Join Kossuth Lajos utca and continue out to the Small Boulevard.

❺ Turn right on to Múzeum körút. Stop for a turn around the Hungarian National Museum (▷ 68) on the left-hand side of the road.

WALK

AROUND BELVÁROS

Shopping

AJKA KRISTÁLY
www.ajka-crystal.hu
Shop offering fine crystal ware, as well as Zsolnay porcelain.
➕ D9 ✉ V, Kossuth Lajos utca 10 ☎ 328 0844
🕐 Mon–Fri 10–6, Sat 10–1
🚇 Ferenciek tere 🚌 Bus: 7, 8, 15, 78, 173; tram: 2, 2A

BELVÁROSI AUKCIÓSHÁZ
www.belvarosiaukcioshaz.hu
This shop—one of a chain with outlets all over the city—sells antiques, furniture and paintings, and holds auctions twice a week. For details of the next auction, check out the website www.bav.hu.
➕ D9 ✉ V, Váci utca 36
☎ 267 3539 🕐 Mon–Fri 10–6, Sat 10–4 🚇 Ferenciek tere 🚌 Bus 7, 8, 15, 78, 173; tram: 2, 2A

LA BOUTIQUE DES VINS
One of several outlets run by these producers of premium wine from regions all over Hungary. There are also imported wines on sale (although these are predictable), and there is a shipping service.
➕ C8 ✉ V, József Attila utca 12 ☎ 317 5919
🕐 Mon–Fri 10–8, Sat 10–3
🚇 Vörösmarty tér 🚌 Bus: 4, 15

CHRISTMAS MARKET
In December, Vörösmarty tér is filled with around 100 stalls selling quaint Christmas gifts, handcrafted from wood and glass. You can also buy cups of hot mulled wine.
➕ C8 ✉ V, Vörösmarty tér
🕐 Throughout Dec
🚇 Vörösmarty tér

CSÓK ISTVÁN GALÉRIA
www.kepcsarnok.hu
At this gallery on the corner of Pesti Barnabás utca, you can view and buy works of contemporary Hungarian art, as well as antiques.
➕ D9 ✉ V, Váci utca 25
☎ 318 2592 🕐 Sun–Fri 10–8, Sat 10–1 🚇 Ferenciek

HEREND

The village of Herend lies to the north of Lake Balaton (▷ 105). Founded in 1826, the manufactory began making fine, artistic porcelain when it was taken over by the ambitious Mór Fischer in 1840, and quickly received high acclaim. Among eminent purchasers of Herend pieces were Queen Victoria and Ferenc József I, both of whom have patterns named after them. Today it exports to over 60 countries.

---

tere 🚌 Bus: 7, 8, 15, 78, 173; tram: 2, 2A

FOLKART CENTRUM
www.folkartcentrum.hu
This is the country's largest folk-art shop, selling a massive selection of handicrafts—including embroidery, traditional costumes, pottery, wooden toys, porcelain and other gifts.
➕ D9 ✉ V, Váci utca 58
☎ 318 5840 🕐 Daily 10–7
🚌 Bus: 5, 8, 15; tram: 2, 2A

HERENDI PORCELÁN
A shop specializing in pieces of Herend (▷ panel). This fine porcelain has a long and distinguished tradition and is highly regarded around the world. There is another outlet at Kígyó utca 5.
➕ C8 ✉ V, József nádor tér 11 ☎ 317 2622
🕐 Mon–Fri 10–6, Sat–Sun 9–1 🚇 Vörösmarty tér
🚌 Bus: 4, 15

HUGO BOSS
www.hugoboss.com
Stocks expensive clothes by the renowned international fashion house.
➕ D8 ✉ V, Deák Ferenc utca 15 ☎ 459 8090
🕐 Mon–Fri 10–6, Sat 10–1
🚇 Deák tér 🚌 Bus: 15

JACKPOT AND COTTONFIELD
www.cottonfield.dk
This shop stocks quality clothes for men

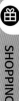

and women. There are more stores in the Westend City Center (▷ 59) and Mammut (▷ 34) malls.

🚇 D8 ✉ V, Váci utca 9
☎ 332 9979 🕐 Mon–Sat 10–7, Sun 10–3
Ⓜ Vörösmarty tér 🚊 Tram: 2, 2A

NAGYCSARNOK

www.csapi.hu

Perhaps the city's most famous and vibrant place to shop, this huge indoor market hall has a bustling atmosphere and wares ranging from fresh food and wine to glass and embroidered lace.

🚇 D10 ✉ IX, Vámház körút 1–3 🕐 Mon 6–5, Tue–Fri 6–6, Sat 6–2 (closed Sun, national hols)
🚎 Trolley-bus: 8; tram: 2, 47, 49

PRÉS HÁZ WINE SHOP AND MUSEUM

www.preshaz.hu

This wine shop and museum stocks over 300 Hungarian wines from seven regions. It organizes regular wine-tasting sessions, and showcases traditional items relating to viniculture.

🚇 C8 ✉ V, Váci utca 10
☎ 266 1100 🕐 Mon–Fri 10–7, Sat 10–6
Ⓜ Vörösmarty tér

SALAMANDER CIPŐ

www.salamander.hu

This exclusive retailer

of leather handbags and shoes has several outlets in the capital, including three on Váci utca alone (also at Nos. 23 and 28). The quality is top-notch, although the goods are expensive by Hungarian standards.

🚇 C8 ✉ V, Váci utca 8
☎ 434 5571 🕐 Mon–Fri 10–7, Sat 10–5, Sun 11–5
Ⓜ Vörösmarty tér

SZAMOS MARCIPÁN

www.szamosmarcipan.hu

Szamos supplies marzipan to confectioners all over the city. In its small shop just off Váci utca you can buy a range of chocolate-covered marzipan

ZSOLNAY

The Zsolnay factory in Pécs was established in 1852 by Miklós Zsolnay. His son Vilmos experimented with different types of clay and glaze, and devised the unique lustrous finish associated with many Zsolnay pieces. In addition to its ornamental and tableware, Zsolnay gained renown for its so-called pyrogranite ceramic for use on buildings; it is this that is so recognizable in the bright and patterned roofs of buildings like the Mátyás Church (▷ 30).

products, many sculpted into the shape of figurines or fruits. In summer, ice cream is also sold here.

🚇 D9 ✉ V, Párisi utca 3
☎ 317 3643 🕐 Daily 10–7
Ⓜ Ferenciek tere
🚌 Bus: 15

TISZA CIPŐ

www.tiszacipo.hu

Once a state-owned shoe shop purveying mass-produced trainers, this store has reinvented itself and now sells clothes as well as shoes. All items are made in Hungary, and the shop is now extremely popular with younger buyers.

🚇 D8 ✉ VII, Károly körút 1
☎ 266 3055 🕐 Mon–Fri 10–7, Sat 9–1 Ⓜ Astoria
🚌 Bus: 7, 7A; trolley-bus: 74; tram: 47, 49

ZSOLNAY PORCELÁN

www.zsolnay.hu

Outlet selling the distinctive porcelain produced at the famous manufactory in Pécs (▷ panel). There is another outlet at Kossuth Lajos utca 10.

🚇 D9 ✉ V, Kígyó utca 4
☎ 318 3712 🕐 Mon–Fri 10–6, Sat 10–1 Ⓜ Ferenciek tere 🚌 Bus: 7, 8, 15, 78, 173; tram: 2, 2A

Entertainment and Nightlife

ALCATRAZ
www.alcatraz.hu
This underground club and restaurant has a prison theme, with parts of the bar divided between cells. There is live music from 9 during the week and from 10 at weekends.

🔢 E8 ✉ VII, Nyár utca 1 ☎ 478 6010 🕐 Mon–Wed 6–2, Thu–Sat 6–4 🚇 Blaha Lujza tér 🚌 Bus: 7, 7A, 73, 78, 173; trolley-bus: 74; tram: 4, 6

CLUB SEVEN
www.clubseven.hu
It's fairly inconspicuous from the street outside, but Club Seven is a classy cocktail-style bar behind red velvet curtains. There is a stage hosting live jazz, dance and erotic acts, and regular theme nights.

🔢 E8 ✉ VII, Akácfa utca 7 ☎ 478 9030 🕐 Daily 10–5 🚇 Blaha Lujza tér 🚌 Bus: 7, 7A, 73, 78, 173; trolley-bus: 74; tram: 4, 6

FAT MO'S
www.fatmo.hu
Popular with the younger crowd and ex-pats, Fat Mo's is a cellar bar that takes for its theme the era of prohibition in America. There is a snack menu, and DJs play at the weekends.

🔢 D9 ✉ V, Nyáry Pál utca 11 ☎ 267 3199 🕐 Sun–Wed 6–2, Thu–Sat 6–4 🚇 Ferenciek tere 🚌 Bus: 5, 8, 15; tram: 2, 2A

GÖDÖR KLUB
www.godorklub.hu
On the site originally earmarked for the Hungarian National Theatre (before political in-fighting put a stop to the project after the foundations had already been dug—hence the name, which means 'pit'), this is an atmospheric venue for live music and other events. Concerts take place beneath a centrepiece lake with a glass bottom. There is also a bar and café.

🔢 D8 ✉ V, Erzsébet tér ☎ 20 201 3868 🕐 Daily 12–late 🚇 Deák tér

---

DANCE HOUSE
During the communist period, the dance-house (*táncház*) movement grew. This stemmed from a wish to galvanize national identity and culture. People trawled the countryside for examples of traditional dance and music, and then hosted events and classes in urban cultural areas in an attempt to prevent them from dying out. Such dance-house events still take place—you can find more information on www.tanchaz.hu—while there are also traditional performances at the National Dance Theatre.

IRISH CAT
www.irishcat.hu
There's plenty about this pub that's Irish (whisky, ale, music and events) and plenty that isn't (a selection of pizzas, Hungarian dishes, fruit brandy and retro parties).

🔢 E9 ✉ V, Múzeum körút 41 ☎ 266 4085 🕐 Daily 11am–2am 🚇 Kálvin tér 🚌 Bus: 9; tram: 47, 49

JANIS' PUB
www.janispub.hu
Another well-established 'traditional' Irish pub named after legendary singer Janis Joplin. Good selection of whiskies.

🔢 D9 ✉ V, Királyi Pál utca 8 ☎ 266 2619 🕐 Daily 4–2 🚇 Kálvin tér 🚌 Bus: 9, 15; tram: 47, 49

JAZZ GARDEN
www.jazzgarden.hu
Excellent and highly atmospheric jazz club featuring international and local musicians. The interior has been decorated to give it the feel of a courtyard under a starry night sky.

🔢 D9 ✉ V, Veres Pálné utca 44A ☎ 266 7364 🕐 Daily 6–2 🚇 Kálvin tér 🚌 Bus: 9; tram: 47, 49

MŰVÉSZETEK PALOTÁJA
www.mupa.hu
The riverside Palace of Arts is the city's main concert hub, and has excellent acoustics and

seating for almost 2,000 people. It houses the Ludwig Museum of Modern Arts.

F12 IX, Komor Marcell utca 1 555 3300 Box office: Mon–Fri 1–6, Sat–Sun 10–6 Bus: 54; tram: 1, 2, 24

NEMZETI SZÍNHÁZ

www.nemzetiszinhaz.hu
After many years of controversy (culminating in the abandonment of the original project in Erzsébet tér), the modern Hungarian National Theatre finally opened in 2002. It showcases performances of Hungarian drama.

F12 IX, Bajor Gizi

park 1 476 6800 Box office: Mon–Fri 10–6, Sat–Sun 2–6 Bus: 23, 54; tram: 1, 2, 24

OLD MAN'S MUSIC PUB

www.oldmans.hu
This small pub hosts live music daily between 9 and 11. It also serves food.

E8 VII, Akácfa utca 13 322 7645 Daily 3–4 Blaha Lujza tér Bus: 7, 7A, 73, 78, 173; trolley-bus: 74; tram: 4, 6

PARIS, TEXAS

This is one of the leading bars on Ráday utca, a stretch that has emerged in recent

years as one of the city's nightlife hot spots.

E10 IX, Ráday utca 22 218 0570 Mon–Fri 10am–3am, Sat–Sun 1pm–3am Kálvin tér Bus: 9; tram: 47, 49

SZÓDA

www.szoda.com
A recent addition to the night scene, Szóda is a courtyard bar which also has a cellar space for music and dancing. The retro design includes leather couches and rows of soda bottles.

E8 VII, Wesselényi utca 18 461 0007 Daily 8–5 Astoria Bus: 9; trolley-bus: 74; tram: 47, 49

Restaurants

PRICES

Prices are approximate, based on a 3-course meal for one person.

€€€	over 5,000Ft
€€	3,000–5,000Ft
€	under 3,000Ft

ADMIRÁL (€€)

Decorated to resemble the inside of a ship, the Admirál stands by the river opposite Gellért Hill. It specializes in dishes of river fish.

D9 V, Belgrád rakpart

30 318 0723 Daily 12–11 Bus: 15; tram: 2, 2A

ARANY BÁRÁNY (€€)

www.aranybaranyetterem.hu
Located behind Vörösmarty tér, beside the British Embassy, this restaurant serves traditional Hungarian and international cuisine, and has a good range of lamb dishes.

C8 V, Harmincad utca 4 317 2703

Daily 12–12 Vörösmarty tér Bus: 4, 15

BELCANTO (€€€)

www.belcanto.hu
The Belcanto, near the State Opera House, is famous for its staff rather than its international food—the waiters regularly break into strains of classical music as entertainment.

D7 VI, Dalszínház utca 8 269 2786 Daily 12–3, 6–2 Opera Bus: 4

FAKANÁL (€)

www.fakanaletterem.hu
This self-service brasserie on the top floor of the Great Market Hall (▷ 75) has excellent-value Hungarian cuisine.

🔡 D9 ☒ IX, Vámház körút 1–3 ☎ 217 7860 ⏲ Mon–Fri 10–5, Sat 10–2 🚌 Bus: 15; trolley-bus: 83; tram: 2, 2A, 47, 49

FATÁL (€€)

Just off Váci utca (▷ 72), the Fatál—meaning 'wooden plate'—is a busy cellar restaurant serving heaving mounds of hearty traditional fare. Given the size of the portions, the value is superb; the portly waiters clearly enjoy their food too.

🔡 D9 ☒ V, Váci utca 67 ☎ 266 2607 ⏲ Daily 11.30–2 🚌 Bus: 15; tram: 2, 2A, 47, 49

KÁRPÁTIA (€€€)

www.karpatia.hu
The Kárpátia can justly stake a claim to being the most beautiful restaurant in the city. Occupying part of the former presbytery of the adjacent Franciscan church, its walls are smothered with historical paintings dating to the 1920s. There is good-quality gypsy music each evening, and you can choose from the brasserie at the front or the main

restaurant. However, the traditional Hungarian food is can be patchy.

🔡 D9 ☒ V, Ferenciek tere 7–8 ☎ 317 3596 ⏲ Daily 11–11 🚇 Ferenciek tere 🚌 Bus: 7, 73, 78, 173

MÁTYÁS PINCE (€€€)

www.matyaspince.hu
The enormous Mátyás pince has a Renaissance theme, with waiters dressed in period costume. Its size makes it popular with coach parties. Traditional cuisine includes fish soup made from carp and Hungarian strudels. Gypsy musicians play both at lunchtime and in the evening.

🔡 D9 ☒ V, Március 15 tér

DOBOS CAKE

The Dobos Cake is lauded by confectioners worldwide. It was the creation of Hungarian pâtissier József Dobos in 1884, and Emperor Ferenc József and his wife were among the first to taste it. The cake consists of five layers of vanilla or lemon sponge spread with chocolate buttercream and topped with caramel. It was unusual both in its simplicity and its use of buttercream (rather than the more familiar whipped cream), and was an immediate hit in Europe.

7–8 ☎ 266 8008 ⏲ Daily 11–12 🚇 Ferenciek tere 🚌 Bus: 5, 8; tram: 2, 2A

MÚZEUM (€€€)

www.muzeumkavehaz.hu
The Múzeum—named after the Hungarian National Museum next door—is a classy and imposing café and restaurant that has been open since 1885. Its ceiling is adorned with a mural by the master Historicist artist Károly Lotz. The food is mainly traditional, although there are also Mediterranean dishes.

🔡 E9 ☒ VIII, Múzeum körút 12 ☎ 338 4221 ⏲ Mon–Sat 12–12 🚇 Kálvin tér 🚌 Tram: 47, 49

NAGYI PALACSIN-TÁZÓJA (€)

www.nagyipali.hu
One of several branches of this chain of pancake restaurants. There's a wide choice of both savoury and sweet crêpes.

🔡 D8 ☒ V, Petőfi Sándor utca 17–19 ☎ 212 4866 ⏲ 24 hours 🚇 Ferenciek tere 🚌 Bus: 15

NEW YORK KÁVÉHÁZ (€€€)

www.newyorkpalace.hu
The New York Café was once a famed literary coffeehouse, frequented by great 19th-century writers. After a massive programme of

refurbishment, it reopened recently as part of the Boscolo Hotel.
F8 VII, Erzsébet körút 9–11 886 6111 Daily 10am–midnight Blaha Lujza tér Bus: 7, 7A, 73, 78, 173; trolley-bus: 74; tram: 4, 6

PATA NEGRA (€)
www.patanegra.hu
This restaurant is relatively new to the scene, and offers good Spanish cuisine (including tapas), cheeses and an excellent selection of Spanish wines. It has a brick interior and looks on to Kálvin tér.
E9 IX, Kálvin tér 8 215 5616 Mon–Wed 11am–midnight, Thu–Fri 11am–1am, Sat noon–1am, Sun 12–12 Kálvin tér Trolley-bus: 83; tram: 47, 49

PESTI LÁMPÁS (€€€€)
www.pestilampas.hu
Situated inside the elegant Ybl Palace, this coffeehouse, restaurant and gallery serves both traditional and international food. There is also a pleasant courtyard.
D9 V, Károlyi Mihály utca 12 266 9566 Mon–Sat 10am–midnight, Sun 6pm–midnight Ferenciek tere Bus: 5, 8, 112

SPINOZA CAFÉ (€€)
www.spinozahaz.hu
Located in the Jewish district, the Spinoza—named after the 17th-century Dutch philosopher—is a café and restaurant that harks back to the atmosphere of turn-of-the-century Holland. The food is international.
D8 VII, Dob utca 15 413 7488 Daily 11–11 Astoria Bus: 9; trolley-bus: 74; tram: 47, 49

SPOON–THE BOAT (€€€€)
www.spooncafe.hu
The Spoon is located aboard a permanently moored boat on the Pest side of the river near the Intercontinental Hotel, and offers a romantic setting with beautiful views. There is a wide selection of international dishes, including a good vegetarian selection.
C8 V, on the Danube near the Chain Bridge (outside the Intercontinental Hotel) 411 0913 Daily 12–12 Bus: 105, 16, red 4; tram: 2, 2A

GERBEAUD

The super-elegant Gerbeaud (www.gerbeaud.hu) is the best-known café in Budapest. The owner after which it is named—Emil Gerbeaud—was a late-19th-century Swiss pâtissier who attracted people from miles around to sample his sweet creations. Be sure to try one of the specialties of the house such as the Esterházy or Dobos cakes (▷ panel, 81).
C8 V, Vörösmarty tér 7 429 9000 Daily 9–9 Vörösmarty tér Bus: 4; tram: 2, 2A

TRATTORIA TOSCANA (€€)
www.toscana.hu
This riverside Italian restaurant serves both main meals and snacks (such as bruschetta and pizza) prepared in an open kitchen. It is located on the riverside, in between the Erzsébet and Szabadság bridges. You can also purchase Tuscan specialty foods and wines from its shop, which is beside the restaurant.
D9 V, Belgrád rakpart 13 327 0045 Daily 12–12 Bus: 15; tram: 2, 2A

Oktogon to Városliget

Andrássy út continues northeast from the Great Boulevard, finally opening into the broad Heroes' Square. Beyond is the city's main park, which contains the Széchenyi Baths, as well as a fairy-tale castle and a zoo with an art nouveau elephant house.

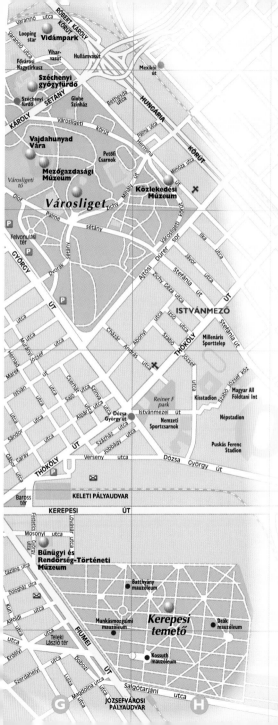

Andrássy út

Statue of Jokai (left); an imposing façade on Andrássy út (right)

THE BASICS

* **E6**
* Shops generally daily 10–6
* Numerous restaurants, bars, cafés
* M1 metro line runs the entire length of the street (between Bajcsy-Zsilinszky út and Hősök tere)
* Bus: 4; trolley-bus: 70, 73, 76, 78; tram: 4, 6
* Very good

TIP

● When you're at Oktogon, keep a look out for the rings attached to the office at No. 13. During the early 19th century, there were plans to turn a stream that ran here into a canal on which gondolas would serve to transport people around the city. The idea never came to fruition, but the rings intended for mooring the boats remain.

Budapest's most elegant boulevard is named after the aristocrat whose brainchild it was. It is arrow-straight, running from the outer edge of the Small Boulevard for about 3km (2 miles) all the way to Városliget (City Park, ▷ 91).

The history In the heady years that followed the Compromise of 1867—when Hungary and Austria became a dual monarchy—Count Gyula Andrássy dreamed of giving the capital a street to rival Paris's Champs-Élysées. The dream became reality when construction began in 1872 on a road leading through Terézváros. During the communist period the avenue was known first as Sztálin út and then Népköztársaság útja (Avenue of the People's Republic); it became Andrássy út once more after the political change in 1990. Since then it has been made a UNESCO World Heritage Site.

A few of the sights The avenue is divided into three main sections. The first (from Bajcsy-Zsilinszky út to Oktogon) is lined with offices and shops, while the other two are wider and characterized by trees and town houses. After passing the State Opera House (▷ 52) and Liszt Ferenc tér, you'll reach the eight-sided junction called Oktogon. Beyond, look out for the Terrorháza (▷ 90), which was once the headquarters of the secret police and now houses a museum. Farther up, there are two collections of Oriental art at the Hopp Ferenc and Ráth György museums.

Hősök tere

The colonnades (left and right) display statues of Hungarian leaders and heroes

The grand Heroes' Square was constructed as part of the millennial celebrations in 1896. It is the gate to City Park, and has traditionally been used as the ceremonial stage for state occasions, including the reburial of Imre Nagy many years after his execution.

Millennium Monument The column dominating the square is 36m (118ft) in height, and bears aloft a statue of the Archangel Gabriel. The angel holds the Holy Crown, which he was said to have preferred to King Stephen in a dream. The plinth is adorned with reliefs of the Magyar tribes—including the main leader, Árpád—who settled in the Carpathian Basin in AD896, and who are the ancestors of today's Hungarians. Running behind the column are two semi-circular colonnades with carved figures of Hungary's leaders. When originally built, the Habsburgs were included but these were later replaced with sculptures of those who fought for Hungarian independence, including Lajos Kossuth. In front of the column is a tomb dedicated to the victims of the revolution of 1956. One of the seminal moments of the revolution came when a huge statue of Stalin that stood at the edge of the square was torn down by the revolutionaries.

Art houses Two neoclassical buildings face each other across the square, the Museum of Fine Arts (▷ 88–89) and the Hall of Arts, which hosts temporary exhibitions.

THE BASICS

🔡 F5

🍴 Café inside the Museum of Fine Arts and the Hall of Arts

🚇 Hősök tere

🚌 Bus: 4, 20, 30; trolley-bus: 72, 75, 79

♿ Very good

HIGHLIGHTS

● The Museum of Fine Arts (Szepművészeti Muzeum, ▷ 88–89)—one of Central Europe's leading art collections
● Hall of Arts
● Millennium Monument

TIPS

● It's best to keep your wits about you when walking in Heroes' Square. Its smooth, paved expanse is popular with skateboarders and trick cyclists.
● The square is at its most atmospheric late at night, when the column is illuminated.

Szépművészeti Múzeum

HIGHLIGHTS

● Equestrian Statue by Leonardo da Vinci (probably the world's only existing statue by Leonardo himself)

● *Sermon of John the Baptist* by Pieter Bruegel the Elder

● *Knife Grinder* and *Water Carrier* by Goya

TIP

● There are free English-language guided tours of the Old Masters collection Tue–Fri at 11 and 2, and Sat at 11.

The Museum of Fine Arts—housed in a building looking like a Greek temple—boasts the country's best collection of art from around the world. Its permanent exhibitions are internationally significant.

Egyptian art The museum's collection of Egyptian art is based on finds made during Hungarian archaeological digs in the 20th century. Among the works are mummies and decorated sarcophagi, the carved figure of Prince Sheshong dating to the 9th century BC, and an ivory magic wand fashioned from the tusk of a hippo around 4,000 years ago.

Classical art This collection focuses upon Mediterranean antiquities, and includes Greek,

Gallery in the Museum of Fine Arts; a European painting; the impressive building is on Heroes' Square; resting on the steps outside the museum (clockwise from left)

Etruscan, Roman and Graeco-Egyptian art. Among the exhibits are vases, marble statuettes and items made from glass and bronze. Look out for the Budapest Dancer (a female figure sculpted in ancient Greece), the bronze Grimani Jug and the statues of leading contemporary Romans.

Old Masters The museum's main attraction is its collection of paintings by renowned masters, the bulk acquired from the Eszterházy family in the late 19th century. Many of the greats are represented: there are works by Renaissance artists like Raphael and Titian, Dutch works by Pieter Bruegel the Elder, a globally important range of Spanish paintings featuring El Greco, Velázquez and Goya, and British canvases by Reynolds and Constable.

THE BASICS

www.szepmuveszeti.hu

🔢 F5

✉ XIV, Dózsa György út 41

☎ 469 7100

🕐 Tue–Sun 10–5.30

🍴 Café facilities

🚇 Hősök tere

🚌 Bus: 4, 20, 30; trolley-bus: 72, 75, 79

♿ Very good

🖐 Permanent exhibitions: free; temporary exhibitions: moderate to expensive

❓ Guided tours available Tue–Sun 10–5.30 by appointment

The chilling House of Terror houses a controversial museum

THE BASICS

www.terrorhaza.hu
➕ E6
✉ VI, Andrássy út 60
☎ 374 2600
🕐 Tue–Fri 10–6,
Sat–Sun 10–7.30
Ⓜ Vörösmarty utca,
Oktogon
🚌 Bus: 4; trolley-bus: 73,
76; tram: 4, 6
♿ Good
💷 Moderate

HIGHLIGHTS

● The Soviet tank filling
the central courtyard
● Reconstructions of the
harrowing prison and tor-
ture cells in the basement
● Wall comprising moving
photographs of some of
the victims of the terror
regimes

The House of Terror is a museum that charts the brutal methods employed by the two regimes that terrorized Hungary during the 20th century, and preserves the memory of their many victims.

History The building on Andrássy út is notorious as the place where first the Hungarian
Nazis and later the communist secret police
incarcerated, tortured and often murdered their
victims. From 1940, the fascist Arrow-Cross
Party rented it as their headquarters and
named the place the 'House of Faith'. After
they were installed in government by the
Germans in 1944, they used the former coal
cellars to hold their primarily Jewish prisoners,
many of whom died here. After the 'liberation'
of Budapest by the Soviets in January 1945,
the communist political police (including the
much-feared ÁVÓ) took over the building, deliberately cultivating its reputation as the 'House
of Horror'. They joined the cellars together,
creating a maze of cells in which to imprison,
torture and interrogate political opponents.
Before the building was overrun by revolutionaries in 1956, the secret police were meticulous in clearing all traces of their activities.

The exhibition The current museum opened
in 2002, and is very deliberately innovative and
evocative; the daring approach divides opinion.
There is video footage and photographs, together with police uniforms, the testimony of
former prisoners and reconstructed torture cells.

Statue of Anonymous *(left); boating on the lake and enjoying the sun (right)*

Városliget

City Park lies behind Heroes' Square and is the capital's main piece of parkland. A haven in summer and winter alike, it has a zoo, circus, amusement park, massive spa complex and romantic castle.

The history The rectangular City Park was once the venue for markets and Diets. It was transformed into a recreational park at the beginning of the 19th century, and was a space used equally by workers who hosted meetings here and nobles who took turns around it in their carriages and finery. Its greatest hour came in 1896, when it was the focal point for the millennial celebrations and held a great exhibition of Hungarian products, inventions and achievements.

The park today The park's main feature is its artificial lake, which is used for boating during the summer and is frozen in winter to serve as a popular outdoor ice rink. A bridge leads over this from the rear of Heroes' Square, and a series of paths run across the park's grass and through its trees. The northwestern section of the park contains a zoo (▷ 92), a circus, an amusement park and the Gundel, Budapest's most distinguished restaurant. Here too are the Széchenyi Baths (▷ 93), where you can take an alfresco soak at any time of the year. The intriguing Vajdahunyad Castle (▷ 94) stands on an island in the middle of the lake, while the Transport Museum (▷ 93) can be found close to the eastern corner.

THE BASICS

☐ G5
🍴 Robinson restaurant & café, Gundel restaurant, Bagolyvár restaurant (▷ 98)
Ⓜ Széchenyi fürdő; Hősök tere
🚌 Bus: 4, 20, 30; trolley-bus: 72, 74, 75, 79; tram: 1
♿ Good

HIGHLIGHTS

● The Széchenyi Baths (▷ 93)
● The lake
● Állatkert (zoo, ▷ 92)
● Vajdahunyad Castle (▷ 94), containing the Museum of Agriculture (▷ 93)

TIP

● During the summer, there are frequent classical and modern concerts performed on a stage in the lake with the castle as a backdrop.

More to See

ÁLLATKERT

www.zoobudapest.com

Budapest Zoo opened nearly 150 years ago, and has striking art nouveau buildings dating from the early 1900s—be sure to visit the Moorish elephant house. The zoo holds over 2,000 species of animal, and has enclosures dedicated to the African savannah and the Artic. The Children's Zoo has a twice-daily show.

🔁 F4 ⊠ XIV, Állatkerti körút 6–12
☎ 273 4901 🕒 Mar, Oct Mon–Thu 9–5, Fri–Sun 9–5.30; Apr, Sep Mon–Thu 9–5.30, Fri–Sun 9–6; May–Aug Mon–Thu 9–6.30, Fri–Sun 9–7; Nov–Feb daily 9–4
🍴 Café facilities 🚇 Széchenyi fürdő
🚌 Bus: 4, 20, 30; trolley-bus: 72, 75, 79
♿ Very good 💰 Expensive

BŰNÜGYI ES RENDŐRSÉG-TÖRTÉNETI MÚZEUM

www.policehistorymus.com

The Museum of Crime and Police History charts the development of law enforcement in Hungary. Among the exhibits are former uniforms, firearms and medals dating from 1848 to the present day, as well as rather gory details of famous murder cases.

🔁 G8 ⊠ VIII, Mosonyi utca 7 ☎ 477 2183 🕒 Tue–Fri 9–5 🚇 Keleti pályaudvar 🚌 Bus: 7, 20, 30, 73, 173; trolley-bus: 73, 76, 80; tram: 24, 67
♿ Good 💰 Free

KEREPESI TEMETŐ

Spreading over almost 55ha (136 acres), the Kerepesi Cemetery is a tranquil spot. Paths lined with chestnut trees lead past rows of graves and mausoleums, many of them holding Hungary's historical greats. Among the many impressive marble mausoleums are those of Ferenc Deák and Lajos Kossuth.

🔁 H8 ⊠ VIII, Fiumei út 16 ☎ 323 5231 🕒 Mar daily 7–5.30; Apr, Aug daily 7–7; May–Jul daily 7–8; Sep daily 7–6; Nov–Feb daily 7–5 🚇 Keleti pályaudvar 🚌 Trolley-bus: 80; tram: 24, 28, 37
♿ Few 💰 Free

A steam train in the Transport Museum

Kerepesi Cemetery

KÖZLEKEDÉSI MÚZEUM
www.km.iif.hu

The Transport Museum showcases some of the items relating to the transport boom of the mid-19th century, given impetus in part by the endlessly energetic István Széchenyi, and culminating in Budapest's underground rail system of the 1890s—the first outside Britain.

🚇 H5 ✉ XIV, Városligeti körút 11 ☎ 273 3840 🕐 May–Oct Tue–Fri 10–5, Sat–Sun 10–6; Nov–Apr Tue–Fri 10–4, Sat–Sun 10–5 🍴 Café facilities 🚌 Trolley-bus: 70, 72, 74; tram: 1 ♿ Good 🎫 Free (permanent exhibitions), moderate (temporary exhibitions)

LISZT FERENC TÉR
This is one of the leading spots for socializing in the city, a long square lined on each side with café-bars and restaurants. It gets particularly busy in summer, when everyone sits at tables outside.

🚇 E7 ✉ VI, Liszt Ferenc tér 🕐 Bars and restaurants generally open noon–2am

🚇 Oktogon 🚌 Bus: 4; trolley-bus: 70, 78; tram: 4, 6 ♿ Good

MEZŐGAZDASÁGI MÚZEUM
www.mezogazdasagimuzeum.hu

The Museum of Agriculture is the largest of its type in Europe, with 12 permanent exhibitions, and occupies the main wing of the Vajdahunyad Castle (▷ 94). Among the subjects covered by the display are Hungarian livestock breeding, the lives of shepherds on the Great Plain, and the history of viniculture, hunting and fishing (including a prehistoric canoe found at Lake Balaton, ▷ 105).

🚇 G5 ✉ XIV, Városliget ☎ 422 0765 🕐 Tue–Sun 10–5 🍴 Café facilities 🚇 Széchenyi fürdő 🚌 Trolley-bus: 70, 75, 79 ♿ Good 🎫 Permanent exhibitions: free; temporary exhibitions: inexpensive

SZÉCHENYI GYÓGYFÜRDŐ
The huge, neo-baroque building near the zoo in City Park holds the Széchenyi Baths, one of the biggest spas in Europe. The archi-

Zeneakadémia (Ferenc Liszt Academy of Music)

Széchenyi Baths

tecture is impressive, and among the nine pools is an outdoor bath.

➕ G5 ✉ XIV, Állatkerti körút 11 ☎ 363 3210 🕐 Daily 6am–10pm 🍴 Café facilities 🚇 Széchenyi fürdő 🚌 Trolley-bus: 72 ♿ Good 💰 Expensive

VAJDAHUNYAD VÁRA

One of the most intriguing buildings you're likely to come across, Vajdahunyad Castle was made from wood as a show piece for the Millennial Exhibition in 1896 and proved so popular that it was rebuilt in stone afterward. Its designer, Ignác Alpár, drew upon over 20 historical architectural styles from around the country. The castle was named after the main part facing across the lake, which was fashioned on the 15th-century Transylvanian family pile of János Hunyadi, the victorious leader of the struggle against the Turks.

➕ G5 ✉ XIV, Városliget ☎ 363 1973 🚇 Széchenyi fürdő 🚌 Trolley-bus: 70, 75, 79 ♿ Good 💰 Free

VIDÁMPARK

www.vidampark.hu

The Fun Park next to the circus in City Park offers some thrills and spills, and includes a roller-coaster and an early 20th-century merry-go-round.

➕ G4 ✉ XIV, Állatkerti körút 14–16 ☎ 363 8310 🕐 Apr–Oct daily 10–7 (summer 10–8). Closed Nov–Mar 🍴 Café facilities 🚇 Széchenyi fürdő 🚌 Trolley-bus: 72 ♿ None 💰 Expensive

ZENEAKADÉMIA

www.zeneakademia.hu

The Ferenc Liszt Academy of Music was founded by Liszt in 1875. The fabulous art nouveau central building on Liszt Ferenc tér dates to 1907. Among those to have taught and studied here are Béla Bartók, Zoltán Kodály, Ernő Dohnányi and Leó Weiner.

➕ E7 ✉ VI, Liszt Ferenc tér 8 ☎ 462 4600 🚇 Oktogon 🚌 Trolley-bus: 70, 78; tram: 4, 6 ♿ Call in advance on 462 4636

Vajdahunyad Castle

A Walk to the Park

This walk takes in Budapest's most elegant avenue, most imposing square and main park.

DISTANCE: 4km (2.5 miles) **ALLOW:** 2–3 hours

START

SOUTHWEST END OF ANDRÁSSY ÚT
🚇 D8 🚊 Bajcsy-Zsilinszky út 🚌 Bus: 4

1 Join the 2km (1-mile) long Andrássy út at its start, where it meets Bajcsy-Zsilinszky út. The Postal Museum has a range of exhibits relating to the early days of the mail service.

2 Farther up on the other side of the road is the beautiful State Opera House (▷ 52). Take a tour or book tickets for a performance later in the evening.

3 Continuing straight on you'll arrive shortly at Liszt Ferenc tér (▷ 93). Move down to its southeastern end for a look at the Zeneakadémia (▷ 94).

4 Just beyond Liszt Ferenc tér is Oktogon, so-named because of its eight sides. Cross over and look out for the Terrorháza (▷ 90).

END

HŐSÖK TERE
🚇 F5 🚊 Hősök tere 🚌 Bus: 4

8 Finish your walk with a drink at the Robinson (▷ 98) or a dip at the Széchenyi Baths (▷ 93). You can take the metro from Hősök tere back to your starting point.

7 Facing the top of the avenue is Heroes' Square (▷ 87), with its Millennium Monument and the excellent Museum of Fine Arts (▷ 88). Cross the bridge behind Heroes' Square and take a stroll around City Park (▷ 91).

6 The stretch after Kodály Körönd has two collections of oriental art—the Hopp Ferenc Museum (No. 103) and the Ráth György Museum (Városligeti fasor 12).

5 After Oktogon, the avenue broadens. You'll find a memorial museum dedicated to Ferenc Liszt at Vörösmarty utca.

Entertainment and Nightlife

BAROKKO
www.barokko.hu
This popular café-bar on Liszt Ferenc tér has trendy decor, serves good snacks and has a basement nightclub hosting live DJs.
🏠 E7 🖂 VI, Liszt Ferenc tér 5 ☎ 322 0700 🕐 Sun–Thu noon–2am, Wed–Sat noon–3am 🚇 Oktogon 🚌 Bus: 4

INCOGNITO
The longest-standing bar on Liszt Ferenc tér, Incognito received a facelift in 2003 and remains a favourite. There is a long list of cocktails.
🏠 E7 🖂 VI, Liszt Ferenc tér 3 ☎ 342 1471 🕐 Mon–Tue 12–12, Wed–Fri noon–2am, Sat 2–2, Sun 2pm–midnight 🚇 Oktogon 🚌 Bus: 4

KAKTUSZ JUICE
www.cactusjuice.hu
This bar aims to capture the feel of an old Western saloon, and serves a wide selection of whiskies and cocktails and sometimes has live music.
🏠 E7 🖂 VI, Jókai tér 5 ☎ 302 2116 🕐 Mon–Thu noon–2am, Fri–Sat noon–4am, Sun 4pm–2am 🚇 Oktogon 🚌 Bus: 4

KARMA
www.karmabudapest.com
Karma has an Asian theme, and includes Indian- and oriental-inspired dishes on its menu. It also has a large range of specialty teas and coffees.
🏠 E7 🖂 VI, Liszt Ferenc tér 11 ☎ 413 6764 🕐 Daily 10am–midnight 🚇 Oktogon 🚌 Bus: 4

KIADÓ
The Kiadó extends over two levels, with ground-floor and cellar areas. It nods towards the British pub in some of its furnishings, and serves food in good-size portions.
🏠 E7 🖂 VI, Jókai tér 3 ☎ 331 1955 🕐 Mon–Sat 9am–midnight, Sun 12–12 🚇 Oktogon 🚌 Bus: 4

PAPP LÁSZLÓ SPORTARÉNA
www.budapestarena.hu
Named after the Olympic champion boxer, and nicknamed 'the pebble', this indoor arena for sports and cultural events hosts concerts by Hungarian and international performers.
🏠 J7 🖂 XIV, Stefánia út 2 ☎ 422 2600 🚇 Stadionok 🚌 Bus: 30, 95; trolley-bus: 75, 80; tram: 1

PUSKÁS FERENC STADION
The country's main sports stadium is named after the great Hungarian footballer of the 1950s. In addition to football matches and athletics events, the outdoor stadium—which seats 69,000 people—is the venue for big concerts and other shows.
🏠 H7 🖂 XIV, Istvánmezei út 3–5 ☎ 471 4100 🚇 Stadionok 🚌 Trolley-bus: 75; tram: 1

STEFÁNIA PALOTA
www.stefania.hu
This old officers' club is now the venue for a cultural centre. Inside is a literary café and a restaurant, and there are regular balls, concerts, exhibitions and a nightclub on weekends. The place also offers a variety of programmes for children.
🏠 H6 🖂 XIV, Stefánia út 34–36 ☎ 273 4100 🚌 Bus: 7; trolley-bus: 72, 74, 75

COMMUNIST REMINDERS

When the Népstadion—meaning 'People's Stadium'—was first erected in 1953, the avenue leading up to it was lined with statues of sport and endeavour in the socialist-realist style. Around 16 of these survive today and can be viewed in the garden of the Puskás Ferenc Stadion (the stadium's name since 2002).

Restaurants

BAGOLYVÁR (€€)
www.bagolyvar.com
'Owl Castle' is cheaper and more relaxed than the Gundel next door. The restaurant takes great pride in the fact that its staff is all female, and that it offers traditional, 'home-cooked' food.
F5 ⊠ XIV, Állatkerti út 2 ☎ 468 3110 ◉ Daily 12–11 ◙ Hősök tere ◙ Trolley-bus: 72, 75, 79

BARAKA (€€€)
www.andrassyhotel.com/dining
The Baraka recently moved to the Andrássy Hotel from the Belváros. The restaurant has art deco styling and a pleasant terrace; the cuisine is highly rated, with plenty of seafood options.
F6 ⊠ VI, Andrássy út 111 ☎ 462 2100 ◉ Daily 12–2.30, 7–11 ◙ Bajza utca ◙ Bus: 4

GUNDEL (€€€)
www.gundel.hu
Gundel is the city's best-known (and most expensive) traditional restaurant. It oozes old-fashioned elegance and

you should dress smartly. As well as the à-la-carte options, the menu also has several fixed-price banquets. On Sunday there's a cheaper brunch.
F5 ⊠ XIV, Állatkerti út 2 ☎ 468 4040 ◉ Daily 12–4, 6.30–12 ◙ Hősök tere ◙ Trolley-bus: 72, 75, 79

INDIGO (€€)
www.indigo-restaurant.hu
This Indian restaurant opened in 2005, and serves good-quality food—including a range of vegetarian options—at reasonable prices.
D6 ⊠ VI, Jókai utca 13 ☎ 428 2187 ◉ Daily 12–11 ◙ Oktogon ◙ Tram: 4, 6

KOGART (€€)
www.kogart.hu
Owned by an art collector, the Kogart is

GUNDEL

The Gundel is Budapest's most famous restaurant, and until quite recently its status as the city's best stood largely unchallenged. There has been a restaurant here since 1894, but it was after the Gundel family took over in 1910 that it began to receive international acclaim. The restaurant's signature dish is the Gundel *palascinta*, a pancake with walnuts and chocolate sauce.

adorned with paintings and has a gallery upstairs. The menu includes international and Hungarian food and there is live jazz music.
F6 ⊠ VI, Andrássy út 112 ☎ 354 3830 ◉ Daily 10am–midnight ◙ Bajza utca ◙ Bus: 4

MAGDALENA MERLO (€)
www.magdalenamerlo.hu
This simple restaurant serves mainly Italian food, although there are also some Hungarian and Czech choices on the menu.
E7 ⊠ VII, Király utca 59B ☎ 322 3278 ◉ Daily 10am–midnight ◙ Trolley-bus: 70, 78; tram: 4, 6

PREMIER (€€€)
www.premier-restaurant.hu
The art nouveau Premier offers contemporary cuisine and a popular terrace.
F6 ⊠ VI, Andrássy út 101 ☎ 342 1768 ◉ Daily 11–11 ◙ Bajza utca ◙ Bus: 4

ROBINSON (€€€)
www.robinsonrestaurant.hu
The Robinson has a pagoda-like feel to it, reaching out into the lake in City Park. It has a relaxing feel in summer and winter alike, and has a wide range of international food.
G5 ⊠ XIV, Városligeti tó ☎ 422 0222 ◉ Daily 12–4, 6–12 ◙ Hősök tere ◙ Trolley-bus: 72, 75, 79

For those willing to explore beyond the capital, there are some lovely attractions within easy reach and worth considering even if you're only on a short break of three or four days.

Aquincum

Women dressed in Roman costume at Aquincum (left); a Corinthian capital (right)

HIGHLIGHTS

● Rare 3rd-century water organ, discovered at the site in the early 1930s
● Small amphitheatre right next to Aquincum railway station
● Mosaics discovered in the governor's palace, some with black-and-white geometric patterns from the 2nd century and others with vibrant scenes dating to the 3rd century

Aquincum on the Buda side of the river was the area settled by the Romans, and it contains a rich collection of remains from that period. You can see the best of them at the Aquincum Museum.

Ample Water The Romans arrived in what is now Budapest in 35BC, using the river as a natural defensive barrier defining the eastern edge of their empire. Celts had occupied this area before them, calling it Ak-Ink—meaning 'Ample Water'—and the Romans adopted a version of the name (Aquincum). The settlement was originally established by civilian workers providing infrastructure and support for the garrison of soldiers in Óbuda, a short distance to the south. The Romans stayed for nearly four centuries, and over that period the town grew in size and importance until it eventually became the provincial capital of Pannonia Inferior.

Aquincum Museum The excellent museum features a large archaeological park containing surviving walls and foundations from the town of Aquincum, including a public baths complex, temples and a courthouse. In addition, a neoclassical building in the middle of the park displays some of the many valuable finds made during excavation of the area. The lapidarium holds over 1,000 stone items such as sculpted grave markers and sarcophagi. There is also a collection of mosaics.

View of Budapest from János-hegy (left); rock climbers descend Palvolgy Cave (right)

Budai-hegység

Behind the Castle District and the other settlements along the river lie the Buda Hills, an area that offers good walking and cycling trails. Buses run into the hills, and there are also a couple of characterful railway lines.

The hills A preferred means of getting into the hills is aboard the Cogwheel Railway. You join this at Városmajor station, to the west of Moszkva tér along Szilágyi Erzsébet fasor. On alighting at Széchenyi-hegy, you can follow walking trails to the Széchenyi Lookout Tower or to János-hegy, the highest of the hills. Alternatively you can join the Children's Railway, whose line runs through popular spots like Normafa lejtő and János-hegy. All the railway staff (except the driver) are children; this apprentice scheme was set up in 1948 by the communist youth movement. Normafa lejtő has wooden tables and is a good spot for a weekend picnic. János-hegy holds the Elizabeth Viewing Tower, which offers beautiful views.

Other sights The Budakeszi Game Park, near Szépjuhászné station on the Children's Railway, contains game species as well as ancient domestic breeds. The Béla Bartók Memorial House (II, Csalán út 29) preserves some of the composer's possessions in the villa he lived in before he moved to America. There are Hungarian paintings and other exhibits at the Kiscelli Museum (III, Kiscelli utca 108).

THE BASICS

✚ Off map to the northwest
✉ District XII
🚌 Bus: 21, 22, 28, 90, 158; tram: 56; Cogwheel Railway; Children's Railway; chairlift

HIGHLIGHTS

● The chairlift running up János-hegy
● The Elizabeth Viewing Tower on János-hegy
● The Cogwheel Railway

Szoborpark

A bust among the trees (left); the striding sailor that is the symbol of the park (right)

THE BASICS

www.szoborpark.hu

➕ Off map to the southwest

✉ XXII, Balatoni út (corner of Szabadkai utca)

☎ 424 7500

🕐 Daily 10–dusk

🚌 Bus from Deák tér at 11 (also at 3 in Jul–Aug)

♿ Good

💵 Moderate

❓ Guided tours available by advance reservation

HIGHLIGHTS

● Republic of Councils Monument—the famous striding, open-shirted sailor that adorns most of the park's promotional literature
● Béla Kun Memorial
● Marx and Engels statues
● Workers' Movement Memorial—a pair of hands enveloping a red orb

Unlike many other countries from the former eastern bloc, Hungary preserved rather than destroyed the statues that once looked over its squares and boulevards. They now stand in Statue Park.

The park Statue Park was opened in 1993 on the second anniversary of the departure of Soviet troops from Hungary. There are 42 works on display, gathered from the city's streets and varying from enormous statues to small reliefs or busts. You'll find tributes to Marx and Engels, as well as one to Lenin that used to stand on the edge of City Park; Stalin, however, is not represented because the only statue of him was destroyed by a crowd during the 1956 Revolution. A statue of a Soviet soldier near the entrance once guarded the base of the Freedom Monument (▷ 46). There is also a memorial to Béla Kun by Imre Varga. Kun was leader of the 1919 communist regime called the Republic of Councils; in revenge for a failed anti-communist coup he executed almost 600 people during what came to be known as the 'Red Terror'.

The shop While a museum shop would not usually merit a mention, the one here definitely deserves a browse. You'll find an intriguing range of fun souvenirs, including original Soviet medals, models of Trabant cars, recordings of famous songs of the communist movement and a can purporting to contain the 'last breath of communism'.

Excursions

ESZTERGOM

Standing on the Danube Bend, Esztergom was once the country's most important city.

It was the royal capital until the 13th century (when Béla IV made Buda the seat of power), and was where King Stephen was crowned. It remains the centre of the Roman Catholic Church in Hungary, and it is appropriate that the basilica is the largest in the country. The cathedral's treasury holds a dazzling array of religious items, the oldest dating back to the time of the Árpáds. Nearby is the Royal Palace, where King Stephen is said to have been born.

THE BASICS

Distance: 56km (35 miles)
Journey Time: 1.5 hours by train and by coach, 3.5 hours by boat (May–Sep weekends only, Jun–Aug daily)
🚌 Coach from Árpád híd
🚆 From Nyugati Station
⛴ From Vigadó tér pier
ℹ Gran Tours, Széchenyi tér 25 ☎ (33) 313 756

LAKE BALATON

The largest freshwater lake in Central Europe lies southwest of the capital. It measures nearly 80km (50 miles) in length, and is often referred to as the 'Hungarian sea'.

Under communism, Lake Balaton's beaches and opportunities for water sports made it the most popular destination for Hungarians to take their summer holidays, and it remains the leading spot for domestic tourism. Its two sides are very different in character. The southern shore is the place for partying, with the main town of Siófok well served with nightclubs, restaurants and resort hotels. The northern shore is prettier and more cultured; Keszthely is a university town with a castle, Tihany has pretty fishermen's cottages and a medieval abbey church, and the plateau of Badacsony is a wonderful backdrop for wine tasting.

THE BASICS

Distance: 89km (55 miles)
Journey Time: 1 hour by train, 2 hours by coach
🚌 Coach from Népliget
🚆 From Déli Station
ℹ Víztorony (water tower), Siófok ☎ (84) 310 117

FARTHER AFIELD

EXCURSIONS

THE BASICS

Distance: 19km (12 miles)
Journey Time: 40 mins by HÉV, 1.5 hours by boat, 30 mins by coach
🚌 Coach from Árpád híd
🚆 HÉV from Batthyány tér
🚢 From Vigadó tér pier
ℹ️ Dumtsa Jenő utca 22
☎ (26) 317 965

SZENTENDRE

Szentendre (meaning 'St. Andrew') is probably the prime excursion point for tourists venturing beyond the capital; the most enjoyable way to reach it is on the ferry, although it's a short drive or trip aboard the HÉV suburban railway.

In the early 20th century, there was an artists' colony here and painters still draw inspiration from its river views and cobbled streets. The town has a good number of museums and galleries, including a Marzipan Museum and an exceptional Open-Air Ethnographic Museum that showcases traditional architecture from regions all over the country. To the south of the town are the remains of a Roman military camp.

THE BASICS

Distance: 30km (19 miles)
Journey Time: 45 mins by train, 1 hour by coach, 3 hours by boat
🚌 Coach from Árpád híd
🚆 From Nyugati Station
🚢 From Vigadó tér pier
ℹ️ Rév utca 15
☎ (26) 398 160

VISEGRÁD

Farther around the Danube Bend is Visegrád, and it is lucky enough to enjoy a position that affords stunning views of the river.

In the 14th century, this town became the royal seat under King Károly Robert. Subsequent kings enlarged and improved upon the royal palace; a visitor during the reign of King Mátyás described it as 'paradise on earth'. Over the years, however, its faded stonework became buried and some even questioned the existence of the legendary palace. However, the site was finally uncovered in the early 20th century, and it has since been reconstructed. There is now a museum inside relating its history. Nearby is Solomon's Tower and above that the citadel.

HOTEL GELLÉRT GYÓGY LLC

Budapest has accommodation to suit all tastes and pockets. You can choose to stay in a luxury spa hotel, a historic hotel dating to the late 19th century, a hostel dormitory or a family-run bed and breakfast in the Buda Hills.

Introduction

The popularity of Budapest as a tourist and conference destination has spawned many good-quality hotels that compare largely favourably with those in the West.

Where to Stay

You'll find hotels in most quarters of the city, but tourists usually restrict their search to four or five spots. The Belváros and just beyond—with the bars, restaurants and shops—contain many of the luxury hotels. There are generally cheaper hotels near City Park, which has several attractions and is within easy reach of Liszt Ferenc tér and the heart of the city. A few hotels—including the famous Gellért—make use of the river views on the Buda side, and there are a couple of surprisingly affordable ones in the Castle District. The best-value and most vibrant of the pensions (bed-and-breakfast guest-houses) dot the Buda Hills, and are perfect for those who wish to escape the crowds.

What to Expect

Apart from in hostels, you can usually expect your room at least to have a television and en-suite bathroom. There is little inexpensive accommodation in the middle of the city—a place calling itself a pension (*panzió*) in Pest will often be more like a mid-range hotel. Budget visitors should seek out the few hostels, or consider booking a private or college room (the latter frequently offered during vacation periods). Accommodation-booking agencies can sort these out for you.

SAVING MONEY

Hotels are at their most expensive in high season (between May and October and at Christmas/New Year) and during festivals or major events. However, weekend-break discounts are common, and for the last couple of years, most hotels have participated in a winter promotion offering four nights for the price of three. Rates will usually drop for stays of several days or for advance reservations.

Budget Hotels

PRICES

Expect to pay under 15,000Ft for a double room per night in a budget hotel.

BÁNKI HOSTEL

www.hostels.hu
This hostel has 23 rooms and is close to the Nyugati railway station. Its rooms are basic but clean, and there are laundry facilities and a TV room.
🔀 D6 ⊠ VI, Podmaniczky utca 8 ☎ 788 1081 🚇 Nyugati pályaudvar 🚋 Trolley-bus: 72, 73; tram: 4, 6

CSÁSZÁR HOTEL

www.hotelcsaszar.hu
Located 500m (550 yds) from Margaret Bridge, this 35-room hotel shares a building with the Komjádi-Császár swimming pool. Each room has a bathroom, TV and minibar.
🔀 B4 ⊠ II, Frankel Leó utca 35 ☎ 336 2640; fax: 336 2644 🚋 Bus: 86; tram: 17

DOMINO HOSTEL

www.dominohostel.com
The Domino has 45 dorm rooms. It is superbly situated on Váci utca and as such is excellent value. Understandably popular with backpackers.
🔀 D9 ⊠ V, Váci utca 77 ☎ 235 0492; fax 216 4733

🚋 Bus: 15; tram: 2, 2A, 47, 49

GOLD PANZIÓ

www.goldhotel.hu
This family-run pension is a short distance beyond City Park (▷ 91) in a quiet residential area. Among its services is free wireless internet access. There are 24 rooms.
🔀 J3 ⊠ XIV, Pándorfalu utca 15 ☎ 252 0470; fax: 251 6282 🚋 Bus: 25; trolley-bus: 74

GÓLIÁT HOTEL

www.gerandhotels.hu
This 30-room hotel stands near City Park (▷ 91). The rooms have a toilet, but showers are on the corridors.
🔀 G3 ⊠ XIII, Kerekes utca

PRIVATE ROOMS

A good way of saving money is by booking a private room in the house of a local resident. Rooms are offered in houses all over the city, so be sure to specify that you want one in the very middle if you want to avoid the risk of being in a shabby area. The following are two agencies that arrange private rooms:
Best Hotel Service
www.besthotelservice.hu
☎ 318 5776

Ibusz
www.ibusz.hu
☎ 485 2767

12–20 ☎ 350 1456; fax: 349 4985 🚋 Bus: 20, 30, 32; tram: 1, 1A

KULTURINNOV

The Kulturinnov occupies a neo-Gothic building facing the Mátyás Church (▷ 30) in the Castle District. Its 16 rooms are very basic, but its position is excellent and the building lovely.
🔀 B7 ⊠ I, Szentháromság tér 6 ☎ 224 8102; fax: 375 1886 🚋 Bus: 26, Várbusz

MARCO POLO HOSTEL

www.marcopolohostel.com
One of the city's best-known hostels, the 12-room Marco Polo in the Jewish District has doubles and quads, each with en-suite bathrooms and TV. The dormitories sleep up to 12 people. There is a cellar bar.
🔀 E8 ⊠ VII, Nyár utca 6 ☎ 413 2555; fax 413 6058 🚋 Trolley-bus: 74; tram: 4, 6

RILA HOTEL

www.hotelrila.com
Southeast of the heart of the city, the 30-room Rila markets itself as both a hotel and hostel. Its wood-floored rooms are cheerful, and range from singles up to dormitories holding five beds.
🔀 G11 ⊠ IX, Fehér Holló utca 2 ☎ 323 2999; fax: 323 2998 🚇 Nagyvárad tér 🚋 Tram: 24

Mid-Range Hotels

PRICES

Expect to pay 15,000–62,500Ft per night for a double room in a mid-range hotel.

ART

www.hotelart.hu
This modern Best Western hotel near Kálvin tér is well positioned and has facilities including a fitness room, sauna, restaurant and bar.

➕ D9 ✉ V, Királyi Pál utca 12 ☎ 266 2166; fax: 266 2170 Ⓜ Kálvin tér 🚌 Bus: 15; tram: 47, 49

ASTORIA

www.danubiushotels.com
The Astoria is based in a graceful turn-of-the-century building on the Small Boulevard and has an atmospheric café-restaurant. Its 138 rooms aren't the biggest, but they are comfortable.

➕ D9 ✉ V, Kossuth Lajos utca 19–21 ☎ 889 6000; fax: 889 6091 Ⓜ Astoria 🚌 Bus: 7, 9, 73, 78; tram: 47, 49

BAROSS

www.barosshotel.hu
The Baross isn't the most central hotel, but is convenient for those arriving at Keleti Railway Station. Bright and modern, its rooms are good value. There are apartments overlooking an inner courtyard.

➕ G8 ✉ VII, Baross tér 15 ☎ 461 3010; fax: 343 2770 Ⓜ Keleti pályaudvar 🚌 Bus: 7, 20, 30, 73, 173; trolley-bus: 73, 76

BURG HOTEL

www.burghotelbudapest.com
Given its location in the Castle District, the 26-room Burg offers attractive value. There is no restaurant, but the rooms are well-equipped.

➕ B7 ✉ I, Szentháromság tér 7 ☎ 212 0269; fax: 212 3970 🚌 Bus: 16, Várbusz

DANUBIUS HEALTH SPA RESORT MARGITSZIGET

www.danubiushotels.com
This 267-room hotel on Margaret Island makes use of three local thermal springs and offers an extensive range of spa and beauty treatments. Its health and fitness facilities are excellent.

TAX

The cost of hotel rooms in Hungary is subject to both VAT (ÁFA) at 20% and a variable local levy called Tourist Tax (IFA), which is currently 3% in Budapest. Those under 18 and over 65 are exempt from paying Tourist Tax. While VAT is almost always included in the advertised room rates, the Tourist Tax is frequently excluded and added to the bill at check-out.

➕ D2 ✉ XIII, Margitsziget ☎ 889 4700; fax: 889 4988 🚌 Bus: 26, 106; tram: 1, 1A

DÉLIBÁB HOTEL

www.hoteldelibab.hu
The neo-Renaissance-style Délibáb has 34 rooms and faces Heroes' Square (▷ 87). There is no restaurant and the rooms are simply furnished, but the prices are at the lower end of the mid-range bracket.

➕ F5 ✉ VI, Délibáb utca 35 ☎ 342 9301; fax: 342 8153 Ⓜ Hősök tere 🚌 Bus: 20, 30; trolley-bus: 75, 79

HOTEL ERZSÉBET

www.danubiushotels.com
Named after the wife of Emperor Ferenc József, the original hotel was built in 1873. The current version retains the original style and has a beer hall adorned with murals. It is well positioned in the Belváros and has 123 rooms.

➕ D9 ✉ V, Károyli Mihály utca 11–15 ☎ 889 3700; fax: 889 3763 Ⓜ Ferenciek tere 🚌 Bus: 7, 8, 73

HOTEL GELLÉRT

www.danubiushotels.com
One of the city's classic hotels, the art nouveau-style Gellért stands beside Freedom Bridge and was first opened in 1918. Its 234 rooms vary in size; those facing the river can be noisy because of the trams running below.

Guests have free access to the adjacent baths (▷ 41).
🏠 D10 ⊠ XI, Szent Gellért tér 1 ☎ 889 5500; fax: 889 5505 🚌 Bus: 7, 7A, 8, 27, 86, 173; tram: 18, 19, 47, 49

MÁTYÁS CITY HOTEL
www.cityhotels.hu
This imposing, neo-classical-style hotel stands beside Elizabeth Bridge in the heart of the Belváros. Its huge cellar restaurant has a medieval theme. The 85 rooms are functional rather than elegant, but are clean and comfortable. Try to book one with a river view.
🏠 D9 ⊠ V, Március 15 tér 8 ☎ 338 4711; fax: 317 9086 🚌 Bus: 5, 7, 8, 15; tram: 2, 2A

MERCURE BUDAPEST CITY CENTER
www.mercure.com
Located right in the middle of the action on the prime tourist street. The hotel's 227 rooms are contemporary in style and there's a bar with a skittle alley.
🏠 D9 ⊠ V, Váci utca 20 ☎ 485 3100; fax: 485 3111 🚇 Vörösmarty tér 🚌 Bus: 7, 73, 78, 173

K+K HOTEL OPERA
www.kkhotels.com
Standing on a street near the State Opera House (▷ 52), the K+K Hotel Opera has 205

bright rooms and facilities that include a bar, bistro, sauna and gym.
🏠 D7 ⊠ VI, Révay utca 24 ☎ 269 0222; fax: 269 0230 🚇 Opera 🚌 Bus: 4

HOTEL PARLAMENT
www.parlament-hotel.hu
Located a short distance to the east of Parliament, this newish hotel has 65 rooms decorated in a trendy, minimalist style, a sauna and a lounge bar (but no restaurant).
🏠 D6 ⊠ V, Kálmán Imre utca 19 ☎ 374 6000; fax: 373 0843 🚇 Kossuth tér, Nyugati tér 🚌 Trolley-bus: 70, 78

RADISSON SAS BÉKE
www.radisson.com
First opened in 1914, the Béke preserves its original façade but has modern amenities

---

BREAKFAST

Breakfast is usually included in the price of a hotel stay—although a few of the upper-end hotels charge extra, so it's worth checking in advance. The fare is generally a buffet spread. The choice varies from place to place, but will always include salami, cheese, bread and cereals, and will often feature fruit, yoghurt and hot options like bacon, scrambled egg and sausages.

---

including a swimming pool and fitness area. Its 247 rooms are a good standard and the Zsolnay Café is a popular spot for a coffee and cake. On the Great Boulevard.
🏠 D6 ⊠ VI, Teréz körút 43 ☎ 889 3900 🚇 Nyugati pályaudvar 🚌 Bus: 6, 26, 91, 191; trolley-bus: 72, 73; tram: 4, 6

HOTEL STADION
www.danubiushotels.com
The Stadion is in the city's Sports District, near the Ferenc Puskás Stadium. It isn't the prettiest accommodation, but its 379 rooms have all you need and other facilities include a swimming pool, sauna, fitness room and beauty salon.
🏠 J7 ⊠ XIV, Ifjúság útja 1–3 ☎ 889 5200; fax: 889 5252 🚇 Stadionok 🚌 Bus: 95; trolley-bus: 75, 77; tram: 1, 1A

ZARA BOUTIQUE HOTEL
www.boutiquehotelzara.com
In a superb position just off the southern end of Váci utca (▷ 72), near the Great Market Hall (▷ 75), the Zara draws on Oriental influences in its furnishings. Its compact rooms offer flat-screen TVs and internet access.
🏠 D10 ⊠ V, Só utca 6 ☎ 357 6170; fax: 357 6171 🚌 Bus: 15; tram: 2, 2A, 47, 49

Luxury Hotels

ANDRÁSSY HOTEL

www.andrassyhotel.com
This Bauhaus-style hotel settled among the villas and embassies toward the far end of Andrássy út has 67 spacious rooms. There is free Wi-Fi access. Baraka (▷ 98) is excellent.

➕ F6 ✉ VI, Andrássy út 111 ☎ 462 2100; fax: 322 9445 🚇 Bajza utca
🚌 Bus: 4

BAGLIONI HOTEL AND RÁCZ THERMAL SPA

www.baglionihotels.com
The Baglioni Hotel in Buda has chic Italian décor and is linked to the adjacent Turkish baths, which have been overhauled to become the city's most exclusive spa. There are 43 rooms and 20 suites.

➕ C9 ✉ I, Hadnagy utca 8–10 ☎ 487 0313; fax: 487 0314 🚌 Bus: 5, 78, 86; tram: 18, 118

CORINTHIA GRAND HOTEL ROYAL

www.corinthia.hu
The lovely Corinthia Grand on the Great Boulevard has 414 immaculate rooms, an impressive marble lobby, a brasserie and sushi restaurant, and a spa next door.

➕ E7 ✉ VII, Erzsébet körút 43–49 ☎ 479 4000; fax: 479 4333 🚇 Trolley-bus: 70, 78; tram: 4, 6

FOUR SEASONS HOTEL GRESHAM PALACE

www.fourseasons.com/budapest/
The Four Seasons occupies the art nouveau edifice built for a British insurance company in the early 20th century (▷ 58). It reopened a couple of years ago after a painstaking renovation, and is now the country's most luxurious hotel. It has 179 opulent rooms, a traditional coffeehouse and fine restaurant.

➕ C8 ✉ V, Roosevelt tér 5–6 ☎ 268 6000; fax: 268 5000 🚇 Deák tér 🚌 Bus: 4, 15, 16, 105; tram: 2, 2A

HILTON BUDAPEST

www.danubiushotels.com
With a daring design that blends tinted glass with the remains of a medieval Dominican monastery, the Hilton stands on the main square in the Castle District and its river-facing rooms offer some of the best views in the city.

➕ B7 ✉ I, Hess András tér 1–3 ☎ 889 6600; fax: 889 6644 🚌 Bus: 16, Várbusz

INTERCONTINENTAL BUDAPEST

www.intercontinental.com/icbudapest
Well located near the Chain Bridge, the InterContinental's upper rooms allow beautiful river views. There are nearly 400 rooms in total; the restaurant has a good reputation.

➕ C8 ✉ V, Apáczai Csere János utca 12–14 ☎ 327 6333; fax: 327 6356
🚇 Deák tér 🚌 Bus: 4, 15, 16, 105

KEMPINSKI HOTEL CORVINUS

www.kempinski-budapest.com
This classy hotel in the Belváros has 335 stylishly furnished rooms, a pair of excellent restaurants and a beer hall, swimming pool and fitness area.

➕ D8 ✉ V, Erzsébet tér 7–8 ☎ 429 3777; fax: 429 4777 🚇 Deák tér 🚌 Bus: 4, 16; tram: 47, 49

Here is key information to help smooth your path both before you go and when you arrive. It gives you all you need to know about local transport, useful websites and the best of the city's annual events.

Planning Ahead

When to Go

Budapest can get very hot in high season (May to September). Autumn is pleasantly mild and the hues of the Buda Hills are lovely, while the Spring Festival is the country's leading cultural event. In December there is a Christmas market.

> **TIME**
>
> Budapest is 1 hour ahead of London and 5 hours ahead of New York.

AVERAGE DAILY MAXIMUM TEMPERATURES

JAN	FEB	MAR	APR	MAY	JUN	JUL	AUG	SEP	OCT	NOV	DEC
57°F	59°F	63°F	67°F	71°F	77°F	81°F	82°F	79°F	72°F	63°F	58°F
14°C	15°C	17°C	20°C	21°C	25°C	27°C	28°C	26°C	22°C	17°C	15°C

Spring begins in late March and lasts until around mid-May. It is characterized by mild temperatures and regular showers.

Summer months are steamy, and it is far from unusual for temperatures in July and August to hit 35°C or higher. Many locals head for Lake Balaton to cool down.

Autumn starts fairly warm before becoming cooler and wetter, with occasional fog. It is an ideal time for cycling or walking in the hills to the west.

Winter temperatures dip sharply from mid-November. December and January are the coldest months. There is snow every year, but it does not last for long.

WHAT'S ON

March/April *Spring Festival*: The main festival of culture, with a fortnight of music and dance events held at numerous venues across the city.

June *Budapest Fair*: Weekend carnival and concerts to celebrate the withdrawal of Soviet troops in 1991.

July and August *Summer on the Chain Bridge*: The city's main bridge is closed to traffic each weekend, and hosts performances of music and dance.

August *Sziget Festival*: Massive festival of popular music on Shipyard Island featuring international acts.

Celebration of Crafts: Workshops and displays of craftwork in Buda Castle. *St. Stephen's Day*: Huge fireworks display by the Danube on 20 August. *Budapest Parade*: Carnival floats that parade along Andrássy út.

August–September *Jewish Festival*: Celebration of Jewish heritage and culture, including concerts in the Great Synagogue.

September *International Wine Exhibition and Fair*: The main wine growers display their wares at Buda Castle; there's a procession and other events.

October *Autumn Festival*: The second of the city's main cultural festivals.

December *Christmas Market*: Vörösmarty tér is filled with stalls selling wooden and glass gifts throughout December. *New Year's Eve Gala Concert*: Feast and ball at the State Opera House.

Budapest Online

www.festivalcity.hu
This website lists up-to-date information about the city's festivals, including precise dates, acts and venues.

www.budapestinfo.hu
You can get an excellent introduction to the city on the website of the Budapest tourist office. As well as providing an overview of the city's history and sights, there is practical information about museums and transport, and links to hotels, car-hire firms and more.

www.hungary.com
www.gotohungary.co.uk
The websites of the Hungarian National Tourist Office (the first international and the second the UK branch) give details of the country as a whole and can offer assistance on getting there and other trip preparations.

www.budapesthotelreservation.hu
One of several websites through which you can search for a suitable hotel in the city. It also gives details on current discount deals.

www.budapestsun.com
Online version of one of the city's leading English-language newspapers, hard copies of which are often available free in hotels and bars.

www.bkv.hu
Useful website covering the Budapest public-transport system. It includes information on routes and ticket prices.

www.budapestfunzine.hu
This is the online companion to the free English-language listings magazine, which includes practical information, details of culture, restaurants, shops, family events and active leisure activities.

USEFUL TRAVEL SITES

www.theAA.com
A great resource for the essentials, ranging from destination information to travel insurance policies. There is also a UK facility for ordering travel guides and maps online.

www.fodors.com
A complete travel-planning site. You can research prices and weather; book air tickets, cars and rooms; ask questions (and get answers) from fellow visitors; and find links to other sites.

INTERNET CAFÉS

There are many internet cafés in the city, including those below. You can find a fuller list on the Caboodle website.

Budapest Internet Café
🔹 D9
✉ V, Kecskeméti utca 5
☎ 328 0292
🕐 Daily 10–10
✋ 150Ft per 10 minutes

Easynet Cyber Café
🔹 B9
✉ V, Váci utca 19–21
☎ 485 0460
🕐 Daily 10–10
✋ 200Ft per 10 minutes

Getting There

ENTRY REQUIREMENTS

For the latest passport and visa information, check your relevant embassy website before you travel.
UK: www.britishembassy. gov.uk
USA: www.usembassy.gov

FLIGHT TIMES

● Flights from the UK to Budapest take between about 2 hours 30 minutes and 3 hours. Direct journeys from New York take a little under 10 hours.

ARRIVING BY BOAT

A hydrofoil service run by Mahart Passnave (☎ 484 4000; www.mahart passnave.hu) operates along the Danube, connecting Budapest with Bratislava and Vienna between mid-April and late October. There are also services to towns on the Danube Bend.

AIRPORT

Ferihegy Airport (BUD) is 20km (12.5 miles) to the southeast of Budapest and is Hungary's main airport. It has two adjacent main terminals, 2A and 2B, and an older terminal from which a few budget airlines fly.

ARRIVING BY AIR

Budapest's Ferihegy Airport (☎ 296 9696; www.bud.hu) is served by many of the major airlines. The Hungarian national carrier is Malév, whose destinations include London Gatwick (and London Heathrow through a code-share agreement with British Airways) and New York's JFK; the company flies in and out of Terminal 2A. Other major airlines use Terminal 2B; among them are British Airways flying to London Heathrow (and Gatwick through a code share with Malév), KLM, Air France, Delta Air Lines and Lufthansa. Budget flights are operated by easyJet, Wizzair and Jet2.

There are several ways of getting from the airport to the city hub, the least expensive by public transport. Bus No. 200 stops outside both terminals 1 and 2, while bus No. 93 runs from Terminal 1 only; both terminate at Kőbánya-Kispest metro station (blue line 3), from where it is a couple of minutes to Deák tér. Bus and metro tickets cost 230Ft (single) at metro station, hotels and other outlets; it's slightly more expensive to pay the bus driver direct. A new, regular railway service

travels between Terminal 1 and Nyugati station and costs 300Ft for a single ticket. If you'd like to be taken direct to your hotel or other address within the city limits, consider the Airport Minibus (☎ 296 8555); you book a ticket at the dedicated desk in the arrivals hall, and it costs 2,300Ft one-way and 3,900Ft for a return (phone 24 hours before your departure to arrange the return pick-up point).

If there are several of you, it can be cheaper per person to take a taxi. The official airport taxi company—with desks at the airport—is called Zóna (☎ 365 5555; www.zonataxi.eu). Never simply hail a taxi from outside the terminals. Your hotel should also be able to arrange a taxi when you depart Budapest.

ARRIVING BY BUS

In Hungary, the national company (operating under the Eurolines umbrella) is Volánbusz (☎ 219 8000), offering long-distance domestic and international services to countries including the UK, Austria, Germany, France and Germany. The UK operator is National Express (☎ 08705 808080). There are three main bus stations in Budapest: Népliget, Árpád híd and Stadion.

ARRIVING BY TRAIN

The three main railway stations in Budapest are the Eastern (Keleti), Western (Nyugati) and Southern (Déli), the first of which receives most international services. Each of the stations is linked to the metro system. The state railway company is called MÁV (☎ 371 9449; www.elvira.hu for timetables and ticketing information). A journey from the UK by rail will take nearly 24 hours and is not cheap. It is more likely that passengers will be arriving from cities in neighbouring countries, such as Kiev, Zagreb, Vienna, Bratislava, Belgrade or Bucharest.

ARRIVING BY CAR

Visitors from Western Europe by car usually travel via Austria, crossing the border at Nickelsdorf (Hegyeshalom on the Hungarian side) and take the M1 motorway for two hours all the way to Budapest. The M5 connects the capital with Serbia (at Röszke, near Szeged). In addition, there are international crossings at the borders with Slovakia, Romania, Ukraine and Croatia. A toll applies on all motorways (highways) in Hungary; you can buy the prepaid toll pass (*vignette*) at many petrol (gas) stations. A four-day *vignette* costs 1,530Ft and a 10-day one 2,550Ft. Remember that in Hungary the legal alcohol limit for driving is zero. Citizens of European Union countries may use their national driver's licences, while other citizens require an international licence. Drivers with insurance from countries that are members of licence-plate agreements with Hungary (including the UK) are covered for liability; citizens from other countries must present a green card (without one, they must take out insurance at the border before entering the country).

Getting Around

BUDGET CARD

● The Budapest Card—a discount card (valid for 48 hours at 6,450Ft or 72 hours at 7,950Ft) giving free access to some museums (where a charge applies) and reductions at selected restaurants and other sights—also allows free travel for one adult and child (under 14).

VALIDATING TICKETS

● You should always validate your ticket at punching machines aboard trams, buses and trolleybuses or at the entrance to metro stations. Inspectors patrol the public transport system to check tickets. If you are caught without a valid ticket (a ticket that has not been punched), you can be fined 3,100Ft on the spot; however, tourists are offered the opportunity to purchase a three-day pass (costing the same) instead of the fine. Inspectors on the metro wear a blue uniform, while those on other modes of transport may be in plain clothes. Be sure to satisfy yourself that the inspectors are genuine before paying a fine; officials will carry formal identification.

METRO, BUSES, TRAMS AND TROLLEY-BUSES

● Budapest has three metro lines (including the first built in continental Europe), 35 tram lines, 14 trolley-bus routes and over 200 bus routes, as well as five suburban railway lines (called the HÉV). All fall under the control of Budapest Transport Ltd (known as BKV). Most public transport runs between the hours of 5am and 11pm, although there are also over 30 night buses (all of which bear three digits starting with the number 9).

● Tickets are valid for use on all modes of public transport within the city limits (although not on the HÉV outside Budapest—you must buy extension tickets for journeys to stations beyond) and are available at metro stations, hotels, newsagents and tourist offices. These can be bought individually (230Ft) or in books of either 10 (2,050Ft) or 20 (3,900Ft) tickets; a single ticket entitles you to one journey without changing trains. In addition, you can buy tourist transport tickets valid for one (1,350Ft), three (3,100Ft) or seven (3,600Ft) days granting unlimited travel within the city boundaries. Although you can purchase tickets from the driver on buses and trolleybuses, they are more expensive than prepaid ones and you will require the exact change.

● The three metro lines are numbered and colour-coded—Metro 1 (yellow) runs largely underneath Andrássy út (from Vörösmarty tér to Mexikói út); Metro 2 (red) is the only line to straddle the river, going from west–east (Moszkva tér to Örs vezér tere); Metro 3 (blue) follows the river in an arc from north to south (Újpest-Központ to Köbánya-Kispest).

● You'll find full information on prices, tickets, timetables and routes at www.bkv.hu. Maps, discount cards and other information are available from Tourinform offices.

TAXIS

Always order a taxi by telephone. Rates offered on pre-ordered cabs are lower than those you will be charged when hailing them from the street. Furthermore—and more importantly—it is unfortunately common for disreputable drivers to significantly over-charge tourists. Only get into a taxi with a registered company name on the side. Check that the meter is reset to the base rate (of around 300Ft in daytime). You should tip taxi drivers around 10 per cent. Some reliable taxi companies are:

City Taxi ☎ 211 1111
Fő Taxi ☎ 222 2222
Rádiótaxi ☎ 377 7777
6x6 Taxi ☎ 266 6666

CAR RENTAL

Budapest is easily navigable by public transport and on foot; driving can be awkward (with many one-way streets and limited parking). However, if you do wish to rent a car you will find all the major international companies are represented. You must be 21 or over, and show a driver's licence valid for a year or more and a passport. Some rental companies will deliver the car to your hotel.

Avis ☒ Ferihegy 1 & 2B ☎ 296 6421; www.avis.hu
Fox Autorent ☒ Nagytétényi út 48–50 ☎ 382 9000; www.fox-autorent.com

OTHER LOCAL TRANSPORT

Budapest also has a funicular railway (Sikló, ascending Castle Hill from Clark Ádám tér; tickets 700Ft one-way, 1,300Ft return), the Cogwheel Railway (running into the Buda Hills from Városmajor station, near Moszkva tér, to Széchenyi-hegy; normal transport tickets are accepted), the Children's Railway (from Széchenyi-hegy to Hűvösvölgy stations; tickets 600Ft one-way, 1,200Ft return).

VISITORS WITH DISABILITIES

While facilities for those with limited mobility are improving in Budapest, it's true that many streets and public buildings remain difficult. Several new buses now have low floors and ramps, including buses 4, 15, 16, 26 and 78. Trams 4 and 6 and trolley-bus 70 also have low floors. Other routes have less regular buses and trolley-buses suitable for disabled passengers; these are indicated on timetables with a wheelchair symbol. For further information, contact National Federation of Disabled Persons (MEOSZ; www.meoszinfo.hu).

TOURIST OFFICES

Tourinform offices (www.tourinform.hu):
☒ Terminal 2B ☎ 438 8080 🕐 Daily 8–10 (24 Dec 8–2; 25 Dec, 1 Jan 10–6)
☒ V, Sütő utca 2 (Deák tér) ☎ 438 8080 🕐 Daily 8–8 (24 Dec 8–1; 25, 26 Dec, 1 Jan 10–6)
☒ VI, Liszt Ferenc tér 11 (Oktogon) ☎ 322 4098 🕐 Jun–Sep daily 10–7, Oct–May Mon–Fri 10–6
☒ I, Szentháromság tér (Budavár) ☎ 488 0475 🕐 May–Oct daily 9–8, Nov–Apr 9–6

Essential Facts

EMERGENCY NUMBERS

- Ambulance ☎ 104
- Fire service ☎ 105
- Police ☎ 107
- International emergency hotline ☎ 112
- British embassy ✉ ÍV, Harmincad utca 6 ☎ 266 2888; www.britishembassy.hu
- US embassy ✉ V, Szabadság tér 12 ☎ 475 4400; www.usembassy.hu
- Irish embassy ✉ V, Bank Centre, Szabadság tér ☎ 301 4960

MONEY

The Hungarian currency is the forint (abbreviated to HUF or Ft). It is circulated as coins up to 100Ft and as notes above that up to 20,000Ft.

1,000Ft

2,000Ft

5,000Ft

10,000Ft

ELECTRICITY

- Current in Hungary is 230 volts AC (50Hz). Plug adaptors are needed to match the standard European two-prong sockets. A transformer is needed for appliances operating on 110–120 volts.

MAIL

Two main post offices in Budapest can be found at:
- Nyugati Railway Station ✉ VI, Teréz körút 61 🕔 Mon–Sat 7–9, Sun 10–5
- Keleti Railway Station ✉ VIII, Baross tér 11 🕔 Mon–Sat 7–9

Smaller post offices are usually open on weekdays between 8am and 6pm. There are sometimes post offices inside large shopping malls. Within Hungary, letters up to 30g cost 62Ft to send and those up to 100g cost 107Ft. A standard letter up to 50g will cost 290Ft to send to Europe and 370Ft to elsewhere in the world; postcards are 140Ft to Europe and 150Ft beyond. You can cash travellers' cheques in post offices, wire money abroad, and settle fines for parking and speeding offences.

OPENING HOURS

- Shops: Mon–Fri 9–6, Sat 9–1. Some food stores and most shopping malls will open longer hours, the latter often including Sundays.
- Banks: Mon–Fri 8–4. Some banks will also open on Saturday, although all are closed on Sunday. Many ATMs are within the bank entrance; you can usually access these out of hours by swiping your bank card through the electronic reader outside.
- Restaurants: Usually open daily 11–11, although it's not unusual for some to close on Sunday and for others to close for a few hours between lunch and dinner.

PUBLIC HOLIDAYS

● 1 January
● 15 March (commemorating the 1848 revolution)
● Easter Monday
● 1 May (Labour Day)
● Whit Monday
● 20 August (St. Stephen's Day)
● 23 October (commemorating the 1956 revolution)
● 1 November (All Saints' Day)
● 25 and 26 December.

TELEPHONES

● The country code for Hungary is 0036, and the city code is 1.
● Budapest phone numbers (excluding the main city code) are seven digits in length.
● For domestic calls from Budapest to areas beyond, dial 06, followed by the relevant area code and then the specific telephone number.
● Calls to mobiles from a landline require the 06 prefix followed by the code of the relevant mobile phone provider and then the specific telephone number.
● The majority of public telephones accept coins, as well as phone cards, which can be purchased at newsagents and post offices.
● The number for domestic directory enquiries is 198 and international 199.
● To call the UK from Hungary, dial 0044, followed by the area code (minus its first zero) and the number required.
● To call the US from Hungary, the international code is 001. To dial Hungary, the international code is 0036.

SENSIBLE PRECAUTIONS

● Budapest is generally a safe city, although visitors should avoid walking alone in some areas beyond the heart of the city after dark. Pickpocketing is common at railway stations and other places frequented by tourists. There are also regular reports of men being conned into buying women drinks in certain bars and then being presented with enormous bills (and being forced to pay by burly staff). Always be sure to order a taxi (rather than hailing one from the street) and check restaurant bills carefully to avoid being overcharged.

Language

Hungarian (Magyar) belongs to the Finno-Ugric group of languages, rather than Indo-European like most of Europe's languages. Consequently understanding and speaking Hungarian poses great difficulty to foreigners even though its spelling is logical. English and German are widely spoken in Budapest and hotel staff may speak several languages. However, learning a few words of the local language will be met with appreciation.

THE BASICS

yes/no	*igen/nem*
please	*kérek*
thank you	*köszönöm*
excuse me	*elnézést*
hello	*szia*
good morning	*jó reggelt*
good afternoon	*jó napot*
good evening	*jó estét*
goodbye	*viszontlátásra*
do you speak English?	*beszél angolul?*
I don't understand	*nem értem*

AT THE HOTEL

single room	*egyágyas szoba*
double room	*dupla szoba*
with/without bathroom	*fürdőszobá(val)/ nél kül*
breakfast	*reggeli*
lunch	*ebéd*
dinner	*vacsora*
how much?	*mennyibe kerül?*
do you accept credit cards?	*elfogad hitelkár tyát?*

FINDING HELP

I need a doctor/ dentist	*orvost/fogorvost keresek*
can you help me?	*tud segíteni?*
where is the hospital?	*hol van a kórház?*
where is the police station?	*hol van a rendőrség?*

NUMBERS

1	*egy*
2	*kettő*
3	*három*
4	*négy*
5	*öt*
6	*hat*
7	*hét*
8	*nyolc*
9	*kilenc*
10	*tíz*
11	*tizenegy*
12	*tizenkettő*
13	*tizenhárom*
14	*tizennégy*
15	*tizenöt*
16	*tizenhat*
17	*tizenhét*
18	*tizennyolc*
19	*tizenkilenc*
20	*húsz*
21	*huszonegy*
30	*harminc*
40	*negyven*
50	*ötven*
60	*hatvan*
70	*hetven*
80	*nyolcvan*
90	*kilencven*
100	*száz*
1,000	*ezer*

AT THE RESTAURANT

restaurant	étterem
menu	étlap
beer	sör
wine	bor
white/red	fehér/vörös
cheers	egészségedre
water	víz
bread	kenyér
orange juice	narancslé
the bill please	kérem a számlát

GETTING AROUND

airport	repülőtér
ticket	jegy
one-way	egy útra
round-trip	retúr
bus stop	buszmegálló
train	vonat
station	állomás
tram	villamos
boat	hajó
entry fee	belépő
free	ingyenes
child	gyermek
adult	felnőtt
where is/are...?	hol van...?
here/there	itt/ott
turn left/right	balra/jobbra forduljon
straight on	egyenesen
when/what time?	mikor?
today	ma
yesterday	tegnap
tomorrow	holnap
how long?	mennyi idő?

SHOPPING

market	piac
what time do you open/close?	mikor nyit/zár?
do you have?	van...?

THE EARLY YEARS

People have lived on the site that is now Budapest for several thousand years. The Romans extended the eastern border of their empire to the Danube after they arrived in the 1st century BC. They remained for four centuries, and Aquincum became capital of Pannonia Inferior.

PEASANT REVOLT

The Peasant Revolt was led by György Dózsa, a man who had received acclaim for his bravery during struggles against the Ottomans. The uprising was crushed, and Dózsa suffered a painful death being roasted on a metal throne and devoured by some of his fellow rebels, who had been starved by their captors.

Orthodox Synagogue; sphinx at the Opera House; equestrian statues on Heroes' Square; roof of the Elephant House at the Zoo; detail of a fountain; the Calvinist Church (left to right)

1st century BC The Romans arrive at what is now Budapest toward the end of the century.

AD896 The Magyar tribes settle in the region.

1000 King Stephen is crowned as the first king of Hungary, and establishes the country as a Christian state.

1241–42 The Mongols invade and devastate the country. King Béla IV fortifies Castle Hill against future attacks.

1458–90 The reign of King Matthias, during which Buda becomes one of the capitals of Renaissance Europe.

1514 The Peasant Revolt (▷ panel, left).

1541 The Turks invade and occupy Buda. They remain for 150 years.

1686 Buda is liberated by an allied European army. Hungary comes under the control of the Habsburgs.

1825 The Age of Reform begins, during which public institutions like the National Theatre and the National Museum are established.

1848–49 War of Independence. Revolution breaks out on 15 March,

during which poet Sándor Petőfi addresses a crowd outside the National Museum. The Habsburgs eventually prove victorious.

1867 The Compromise is agreed, establishing a dual monarchy between Austria and Hungary.

1873 Pest, Buda and Óbuda are officially unified to form the single city of Budapest.

1896 The Millennial Celebrations, commemorating the anniversary of the Magyar conquest.

1944–45 After entering secret negotiations with the Allies, Hungary is occupied by the Germans. Budapest is 'liberated' by the Russians after a savage siege of Castle Hill.

1956 Revolution breaks out on 23 October, but is eventually suppressed by a vast army of Soviet tanks. Hundreds of thousands flee the country.

1989 The fall of communism. Free elections are announced.

2004 Hungary joins the European Union.

2007 Ferenc Gyurcsány is prime minister after leading the socialist-liberal coalition to re-election in 2006.

THE GREAT FLOOD

In 1838, a flood destroyed much of Pest—several monuments bear markers showing the height reached by the waters. In the aftermath, city planners were able to start again and today's layout dates to that period.

TREATY OF TRIANON

Hungary was penalized heavily after its defeat during World War I. The Treaty of Trianon in 1920 stripped it of two-thirds of its territory, something that remains a sore point for Hungarians to this day.

Index

CITYPACK TOP 25
Budapest

WRITTEN BY Adrian Phillips
DESIGN CONCEPT Kate Harling
COVER DESIGN AND DESIGN WORK Jacqueline Bailey
INDEXER Marie Lorimer
IMAGE RETOUCHING AND REPRO Michael Moody, Sarah Montgomery
EDITOR Marie-Claire Jefferies
SERIES EDITORS Paul Mitchell, Edith Summerhayes

First published 2008
Colour separation by Keenes, Andover
Printed and bound by Leo Paper Products, China

A CIP catalogue record for this book is available from the British Library.

ISBN 978-0-7495-5700-3

Published by AA Publishing, a trading name of Automobile Association Developments Limited, whose registered office is Fanum House, Basing View, Basingstoke, Hampshire RG21 4EA. Registered number 1878835.

A03220
Mapping in this title produced from mapping © MAIRDUMONT / Falk Verlag 2008
Transport map © Communicarta Ltd, UK